Second Son of a Second Son

Second Son of a Second Son
Restoration of Life's Challenges

Visit Brian J. Borchers's website at secondsonofasecondson.com

All scripture quotations are from the New American Standard Bible, unless otherwise noted.

Published by: Brian J. Borchers Publishing

Cover Design by: Sara Lynné

Library of Congress Cataloging-in-Publication Data is available.

ISBN-13: 978-0-578-59303-6
Printed in the United States of America

Brian J. Borchers

Second Son of a Second Son
Restoration of Life's Challenges

He Restores My Soul....the Twenty-Third Psalm

Published by Brian J. Borchers
http://secondsonofasecondson.com

CONTENTS

CONTENTS

DEDICATION

There is a phrase in the book that says, "The lady deserved the song." She also deserves the dedication. The one love in my young life, is still the one love in my not as young life.

In the future, if a great book is ever written on grace and kindness, it would include, as its main focus, a chapter on how Peggy has lived her life... with grace and kindness.

Thank you, Peggy, for a wonderful life.

INTRODUCTION

The greatest things are referenced, often. Sometimes, not just through the years, but through the centuries. Such is the Twenty-Third Psalm. It is one of the the most loved, and well known chapters in all of Scripture. In a *Second Son of a Second Son,* I am going to reference just one phrase, "***HE RESTORES MY SOUL.***"

It is a great risk to even attempt to offer any thoughts on something that is already a work of perfection. I have worked in what is called a regulated industry, that is, a company that operates under the watchful eye of the federal government. Risk is not taken lightly. I understand the risk involved in trying to "explain" any passage of Scripture, let alone this one.

I have never thought of myself as one who has heroes. If I did, great trumpeters would be my heroes. I once read that a great trumpeter was asked what he preferred to play, classical or jazz music. He was quoted as saying jazz, because the best you could do with classical music, was to not mess it up. That is the way it is with the Twenty-third Psalm. The best you can do is to try to not mess it up. I'm going to take the challenge. Beaten men do not take a challenge.

My story is not unique. I have not lived a wild life. My history would not be considered exotic. I certainly have had it easier than most people in the world. I was born and raised in America, so why would there be any reason for me to have any complaints, about anything?

One of the great mistakes we make is to compare ourselves to others. We can always find someone better off, or worse off, than we are. We can always find someone smarter, richer, better looking (?), etc., We can always find someone less fortunate.

I share at least part of my story because I know about starting over, more than once. I have not had every negative experience, but I know what it is like to lie face down on the canvas.

On the TV show, The West Wing, Josh is in trouble. His boss Leo, tells him a story, similar to the good Samaritan, about a man who falls in to a pit. In Leo's story, the third person to come by is a friend who jumps down in to the pit. The guy in the pit does not think that is very smart, but the friend says, "It's Ok, I've been down here before. I know how to get out."

Through God's goodness, grace, and kindness, and the same traits in people, I am no longer down for the count. I know how to get out of the pit.

I am not a type "A" personality. However, my brain is frenetic, jumping all over. You will see that in some of the writing. Hang in there. I will usually be able to tie the scattered thoughts together, to make a conclusion that is close to cohesive, coherent, and logical.

I know you are not supposed to write like you talk, but that is what I am going to do. As I write, talking to you is exactly what I have in mind. ***Let's go for a long walk,*** and I'll tell you a story as we proceed. In time to come, I look forward to hearing your story.

PART ONE

IT'S ALL TRAINING

CHAPTER ONE | BEATEN MEN

HOW DO YOU LOSE YOUR SOUL? Your soul is not something like a set of keys or a pair of sunglasses that you inadvertently leave at work or at a restaurant. Ask me how I know about both.

***Have you ever given up**, or been forced to give up?*

How do you lose your ability, your will, (or both) to go on?

How do you lose who you are, or who you were meant to be, who you thought you were meant to be, or who you used to want to be?

What do you do if every preparation you have made, and everything you have worked for, collapses, including you?

Can you recover? How do you recover?

What do you do if you don't know how to recover? What do you do if you don't even want to recover? What do you do if you want to get even, and forget about recovery?

Can a broken life amount to more than just trying to put one foot in front of the other, for just one more day?

You were going to conquer the world, or at least your part of it.

You had the right education, the right training, the right mentors, even some coveted connections. **You were labeled, "can't miss." But then...**

In the clearing stands the boxer...Paul Simon

I was stunned. It hit me like a well measured right cross. The message, was on a plaque, just above the ground. I had taken a road trip to Detroit, to see my youngest sister Barb, and her family. My oldest son, Josiah, was with me.

We arrived early, and had some time to fill. We went to Greenfield Village, next to the Ford Museum, on the edge of Detroit. These days Detroit is on the edge. (More on that later.) My wife and I had visited this attraction, about twenty years earlier. Toward the back of the park, near a plantation, was a quote attributed to Henry Ford. The quote was on a little sign, just above the ground.

Greenfield Village is a nice tourist spot. The Village has moved the homes of many famous people to this one location. Other buildings are replicas, slices of American life through the centuries. I did not see the plaque on my first visit, I would have remembered.

I used to go to Detroit about twice a year. I went once a year for a conference. I also went to the Detroit Auto Show many times. It was always packed wall to wall, everyone trying to picture themselves driving the newest, shiniest, most expensive, sleekest, fastest machines on the road. It was either that, or the biggest, baddest, beast of a truck or SUV known to man. I believe it was held in the Joe Louis Arena.

We're just getting started and you have already seen multiple references to boxing. There is a story behind that. I'll tell you soon.

My sister and her husband had moved from the West coast to the Detroit area to help the company they worked for open their market in greater Detroit. They had a new baby. There were lots of reasons to visit Detroit.

In the early 60's Detroit had the highest per capita income in the country. That is not the case today. Over decades of time, along with massive population loss, the city has seen a reversal of fortune. Many serious, influential forces are working on a recovery plan. I attended perhaps the most important meeting that was held on behalf of the city. I'll return to this thought in a later chapter.

It was just another, ordinary day.

Ok. Back to Greenfield Village and Henry Ford. We were walking along. "I was just minding my own business." (This will be a theme through out the book.) It was a blistering hot day. I don't think we stayed to see every attraction.

I was not expecting anything unusual. That was a major part of what was wrong with my life at the time, and I didn't even know it. Besides, who anticipates God to use Henry Ford to speak in to their life? Is Henry Ford among the prophets? (Borrowed from 1 Samuel 10:12.) Nevertheless, there was something I needed to hear, or see. The words on the little sign read:

Beaten Men Take Beaten Paths

In the past, I had been hit, hard, a couple of times. There had been a complete recovery from the first one. The second one, not so much. Seeing those words, about beaten men, jarred me. I had not yet articulated my outlook. But all of a sudden, I realized, that for some time, I had been going through life as a beaten man, just rolling with the punches. I had a good job, that I actually liked. My wife was still the love of my life. I had not said "no mas" to parenting. (Yes, that would come later.)

It really did stun me. I was shocked. This was completely unexpected. It was out of the blue. I did not say anything to Josiah. We just moved on. I knew something very important had just been communicated. I did not like the message.

That little marker spoke volumes to me. I was immediately able to articulate many things, to myself. I was at a a place in life where the "fight" was not in me. I was not in the ring. I was too tired, too beat up, and too far down in the pit.

I don't like violence. I am a peacemaker at heart. I actually am not that fond of boxing. As I remember it, I was about 12 when I threw my last punch with purpose. Yes, it was directed at my brother. There is a reason I use this blood sport to help tell my story.

Some boxers do not know when to quit. They keep coming back for more, long after they should, sometimes for years. Some of them retire many times. Some are forced to retire because no one in their right mind will allow them to throw, or receive a left jab.

As I said, I am not violent, but I am extremely competitive. The last thing I wanted in life was to be labeled a quitter, someone who gives up, walks away, or does not measure up. If I was not better, smarter, or faster than the next guy, I at least wanted to be seen as better, smarter, or faster. And don't call me mediocre or average. So here I was, at last fully exposed to myself. Every one of my professional bouts had ended up with me on the wrong side of the decision. Some were split decisions, some were not.

The ring and the gloves had been taken from me the last time, several years before Greenfield Village. I had done everything I could to stay active. I had called contacts in several states. I had visited the necessary officials in several states. There were interviews, meetings, and more interviews.

There was a lot of time, energy, travel, and even expense to my efforts. The best I could do, was to hang around the edges for awhile, but the end finally came. I did not respond well.

CHAPTER TWO | 2ND SON OF A 2ND SON

MORRIS HAD DRIVEN HIS MOTORCYCLE out to the west coast as a young man. He had siblings there. He did not stay out there. He came home to Minnesota; to Verndale.

He knew how to train horses. They were one of the loves of his life. He got just good enough grades in school to stay eligible for sports. His kids were not allowed to have the same attitude.

Elaine got really good grades, and took piano lessons. She and Morris grew up five to ten miles apart. Both had the same small town, and small farms as their pre-adult experiences.

They were married on a late November day. The wedding was at the church, (the same church that years later, would alter my life.) The reception was held at the bride's home. Her dad did not attend the wedding. I remember him as a kind, soft spoken man. I was not there for the wedding either, so I did not hear any of the conversations, but her dad, "Grandpa Howard" was strongly opposed to the marriage. He was not ambiguous about it.

He wanted Elaine, (my mom) to go to college. Farming fortunes had changed enough over the decades. He could send her to college. She was only eighteen, just a half year out of high school. Morris (my dad) was five years older.

Both of my parents had siblings much older. Mom had a sister and brother seventeen and eighteen years older. (As kids, the walk to mom's sister's house, for us, was three quarters of a mile by road, or a short walk across a field.) Dad had one brother, six years older, five sisters older than his brother, and one younger sister.

My only older brother Steve was born just short of a year after the marriage.

I AM THE SECOND SON OF A SECOND SON.

I was born, at home, in rural Verndale, Minnesota. I love Verndale. I get there as often as I can, to this day. Verndale is a very small town. It has had a population of about six hundred people for forever. It is what you would call a nondescript place. It sits on Highway 10. There are no stoplights. There are two long, main north/south streets with many short cross streets. The highway runs through the middle of town. The heavily used railroad tracks run between the highway and the city park. Conversation stops for awhile when the trains blow through. They do not stop to unload people or cargo.

When I lived there, the town was surrounded by small family farms. What little industry the area had, was in Wadena, the county seat, seven miles away. If you were going to Wadena from Verndale, the sign said seven miles. If you were going to Verndale from Wadena, the sign said six miles, (or vice versa.) Go figure.

The school sits on the southwest corner of town. Town life revolved around the school, its sports teams and music concerts. The community was always so supportive. I would imagine it is still that way. They still have their own independent school district. I still have the weekly newspaper sent to me.

Graduates who don't leave, like some of my classmates, run the bank in town, teach tech in school in Wadena, teach school in Verndale, become the mayor, farm, drive truck, or build houses.

Minnesota is known for its license plates that say "Land of Ten Thousand Lakes." There aren't any lakes around Verndale. The closest lake (the one I learned to swim in) is 10 miles away. And would you believe it, it is a man-made lake. You have to go east to Brainerd, west to Detroit Lakes, or south to Alexandria to hit areas with a lot of lakes, with famous Minnesota fishing and resorts. We have spent some recent anniversaries in the Brainerd area.

The house I refer to as "Where I Grew Up," was three miles north and three miles east of town. We half farmed. I knew what it was to milk cows by hand and machine, take care of animals, (I am not referring to my brothers,) cultivate corn and bale hay.

We had an assortment of young livestock, sometimes a couple of cows, and up to eight or ten horses. I left home for college just before my dad bought a hundred baby pigs. Some times life does go your way.

I was not properly appreciative of the animals, but did not mind the field work so much. Although I have a great appreciation, and somewhat of an understanding of farm life, the truth is, I would have rather lived in town.

As an adult, on one trip home, I took my two children to a cousin's nearby dairy farm. They were aghast. I actually felt a little bad, that I was raising kids that had no concept of that life. They did not share my dismay.

As a young teen, summers were spent baling hay for area farmers. The work was hard, the weather hot, especially if you were in the hay mow (rhymes with cow). The hay mows were in the second story of the barns. The pay was not going to make anyone wealthy, but there were no "real" jobs for teens available. The lunches served were fit for a king, and meant to provide enough calories to keep a young man going for the rest of the afternoon. A lot of the hay mows had a basketball hoop, that got a lot of use in the winter, once the hay was removed from that part of the building.

I think I was born at home (it was planned that way) because my parents could not afford a hospital bill. When I got old enough to know, I was never given a reason. I did not want to embarrass my parents, or make them uncomfortable, so I never asked. I do know my dad froze, and couldn't cut the cord. He went to the neighbors, and a lady came to help.

At fourteen months I went to live with my aunt and uncle in Mason City, Iowa for about four months. You will come to know him later as uncle Einer. Just a few years ago I found out that I was farmed (literally) out to a family in the church, for awhile. I never asked.

My memory as a child goes back to when I was very, very young. My first memory of my dad is somewhat later. **HERE WE GO….**

I would put my shoes on by myself. I would come to my dad to have him tie them. He would tell me I had them on the wrong feet, (I did not have any other feet.) I really did not know what he meant, it was never explained to me. He would make me take the shoes off. He would throw them in the other room, and I had to go through the entire process again. (He should have named me Edom, Psalm 108:9. You can look it up.) Some days it would take me many times to get it right. Some times life does not go your way.

I had many other, early memories, that had a similar effect on my young mind. He always told me I walked like a cow, which was maybe true. I never knew what he meant by that. I was told my head was way too big. He meant physically, not in a prideful way. My posture was unacceptable, and I talked too fast. Both were/are true. (Slower body, frenetic mind.) As for the walking, I never knew what he meant. I later realized that I walked just like my mom's dad, grandpa Howard.

By the time I was ten I knew my parents' marriage was over. They were not five or ten miles apart, they were five to ten planets apart. They did not get divorced until I was about 30. It was never actually verbalized, but it was branded in to our psyche, by the church, and at home, that if there were unpardonable sins, divorce was very near the top of the list. I don't think there was any improvement in the marriage between years ten and thirty.

There are ten years and four months between the oldest and the youngest of us seven kids. The four boys came first. I am second born, three hundred and seventy-three days after the firstborn. Steve was born early. I was born late. Growing up in our household was easier for all of the boys than it was for the girls. That is an understatement.

CHAPTER THREE | ODD MAN OUT

DAD WAS A FARMER AT HEART. He would have preferred to farm, and nothing else. He never had a good enough start to farm on his own. When he was younger, he never
owned any land. About the time I turned six, he was working on a turkey farm a stone's throw west of Verndale. Before that he worked on a turkey farm a few miles west of Wadena. Both jobs included housing as part of the salary.

I have a genuine appreciation for farming, but I am just not a farmer at heart. Besides, I can not fix anything except breakfast. If you are going to farm you have to have some mechanical ability.

Before I turned seven, the Verndale job came to an end. We moved to the "little green house," just a mile from the "house I grew up in." Somehow, Christmas was still good. I never knew how dad made that happen.

Dad went to Minneapolis, found two good jobs, and after Christmas, we moved to a small community on the north side of the metro. Two and a half years later we moved back to the farm and the green house. Dad kept his jobs in the city and did the commute on weekends for the next twelve years. He would get home some time very late Friday night, or the early hours Saturday morning. He would head back to the city late Sunday afternoon or early Sunday evening.

Grandpa Fred's (my dad's dad) farm was a mile from the little green house. His funeral was Christmas Eve morning, just after I turned eleven. My dad bought grandpa's 120 acre farm from the estate. His six sisters and one brother lived elsewhere, in Minnesota, Arkansas, and the West coast. Thankfully, dad put plumbing and running water in both the green house and grandpa Fred's house. The pump in the green house was a red handled thing you had to prime. The pump at Grandpa Fred's was outside, about thirty feet from the house.

We were all well aware of dad's love for horses. The barn on the green house farm was unsafe and had to be torn down. We had some horses and other livestock in other outbuildings. Dad even bought two small Shetland ponies for us young boys to ride.

The barn on grandpa's farm allowed for an expansion in the animal department. There were now more horses, and more of everything else. I was not good with the horses. I did not know how to let the horse know I was in control. It's probably because I was not in control. I actually was a little bit afraid of the full grown horses.

I do not love horses. I do think they are a very beautiful animal, that should mostly be worshipped from afar. As an adult, on one vacation, my young family spent part of a very enjoyable afternoon at the Kentucky Horse Park. Observation was great, owning them, not so much. Dad loved rodeos. I have been to far more rodeos than I ever dreamed. But then, I never dreamed of going to any.

Most of all, ***dad loved boxing.*** As a young man, he was a boxer. He was a good Golden Gloves boxer. He was five foot seven and thin as a rail. I don't know if he eventually outgrew it, or if mom begged him to quit. I know she did not approve. One of my brothers had a big old fight card poster of dad's that was displayed at his funeral.

Dad bought boxing gloves for us boys. Many a winter weekend was spent with free, compulsory boxing lessons in the living room. We had to not only learn the terminology, but we had to be able to demonstrate it as well. Keep your chin tucked, keep your guard up, don't lead with your right, up on your toes, and a windup is for throwing a baseball, not a punch. Jump rope lessons were a part of the tutorial.

The instructor sat on his knees or haunches, with both palms up, facing us. We had to throw the punches at his palms, with just the right force, had to have the right balance of weight on the right parts of our feet. Did you ever wonder where the saying about keeping up on your toes, originated?

My problem was, I did not want to fight. I know that dad knew it. I knew I was not tough enough for him. I did not have the right aggression. I did not have the killer instinct. I did not have the right follow through in my punches.

Imagine my astonishment, as a father myself, when I came home from work one day, to discover my boys had spent some of their hard earned money, actual, real money, to buy boxing gloves. They were going to do some boxing with some of their friends in the family room. There were no lessons given, free or otherwise. This fad did not last too long.

During the winter dad would take us boys to the Wadena Armory on Saturday nights to watch the local Golden Gloves fights. The White Earth Indian Reservation is a ways north of Wadena. They had a great boxing program, highlighted by the very talented Ballinger brothers. Between the two programs, there were some very good, highly competitive matches. Dad used to ask us to score the fights. Don't ask how often I was right, but I knew enough to know that the official judging was not always correct.

With this pugilistic background to family life, I guess it is not surprising that we kids were allowed to fight with, (meaning against) each other. I don't think I ever fought with Scott, my youngest brother. I fought little with Einer, the third born. Steve and I fought, and Steve and Einer fought.

That is, Steve and I fought if I could catch him. Steve has been a wonderful human being his entire adult life. I was less enamored as a child. I had a short fuse, and felt it necessary to respond when duty called. My mom always said I would have been fine, if everyone would just leave me alone. Looking back I wish we had not been allowed to fight.

I demanded that my boys find a way to resolve their differences without physical altercation. One day one of my boys started a new job with a nice shirt, a tie, and a black eye, given to him, free of charge, by his brother.

It's great to come from a larger family. I did not always think so, as a child. One recent summer, six of the seven of us kids, spouses, and some nieces and nephews were able to spend a week together on some of the islands off the coast of Washington state. My sister Barb and her family have lived on the West coast most of their life. They made the arrangements. The accommodations were large enough that all of us could stay in this great big house, right on the water. Brother-in-law Randy is the best at manning a waterside fire. It was a great vacation. After everyone left the islands, a few of us spent a day and a half in Vancouver.

CHAPTER FOUR | SET A COURSE FOR LIFE

I was glad when they said unto me...Psalm 122:1

There was a constant, a stake in the ground as it were, to family life. Mom and dad were Christians. I am literally, eternally grateful for this. During our "growing up years" that meant going to church, three times a week. It was compulsory. I did not mind going to church. Most of the time I liked it. I just did not always want to go three times a week.

I first prayed the sinner's prayer at the age of five (at family camp.) It was the normal expected thing to do. A few years later, I actually developed a little clearer understanding of the whole process of what it meant to be forgiven. It became something meaningful to me.

This paragraph is critical to the book. We were driving home from church on a Sunday night, to the house of the first turkey farm job. I had probably just turned five. My dad said he thought Steve was old enough to feel God's presence. I immediately knew that Someone was in the car with us. It was the first time I had a personal sense of the Divine interacting with my human being. I never want to underestimate, or undervalue the importance, the goodness, or the availability of the presence of God.

Two verses that highlight this are: The Spirit Himself bears witness with our spirit that we are the children of God, Romans 8:16, and Moses saying, "If Thy presence does not go with us, do not lead us up from here," Exodus. 33:15. (Both KJV).

We were raised in what I considered an extremely strict environment. To our outlook, nothing was allowed. Mom was the enforcer on this. Dad's church attendance faded out in the years after we moved back to the farm. I am very grateful that mom kept us in church on her own. It couldn't have been easy. She never wavered.

We couldn't dance; not that I could anyway. I am a good musician, but I have no rhythm. As student council president my senior year of high school, I was responsible for arranging for the school dances, getting the band, etc. Thankfully my friend Tony took care of most of that for the council. Tony was probably the toughest football player Verndale ever had. Ever.

In fourth grade I got in trouble for suggesting to the public school teacher that Sunday was the first day of the week. The question on a test was, "What is the first day of the week?" (Why was that question asked of fourth graders?) My answer was, Sunday. It was graded as wrong. I had already become aware that I possessed the beginnings of an easy, "I don't have to think about it," sarcasm. I don't think I asked her if she had seen a calendar lately.

When mom heard about the test question, she sent the teacher a lengthy note (which I had to deliver,) complete with Biblical references. The teacher's position was that school started on Monday, making it the first day of the week.

When mom heard about the pep band playing the song, "*When the Saints Go Marching In,*" she did not want me (or the band) playing it. To her it was sacrilegious.

A couple of assigned reading books got banned by mom (at least for a few of us in the class), in junior high no less. I had to read an alternative. One time the alternative was Nathaniel Hawthorne's, House of Seven

Gables. I think that was when I quit telling mom what was going on in school. Mercy.

My friend's parents owned a bar/restaurant in town. Their house was in back of the bar. You had to go through the bar to get to the house. This was not allowed. I confess. Many times, I did it anyway.

I had a guitar. Dale, the friend in question, had a bass. We liked the same music. We had a lot of fun trying to play some of the popular music of the day.

I discovered bowling on an out-of-town basketball trip. Once home, I had to get a special dispensation from a neighboring pastor friend, to go bowling. He had to convince mom that I could go to the bowling alley and still qualify for heaven at the same time. Serious debating skills were needed.

Here's the thing about being raised in a strict family. It's not all bad. Yes, I was troubled, even embarrassed by some of the parental interference. There was a good side of it, in spite of some of the less lenient interpretations of practical Christian life. At least some of, if not most of this thinking permeated a large section of many churches across the country during this time period.

A strong appreciation, a reverence for the Word of God was developed. We did a lot of Scripture memorization. This was sometimes accompanied by contests. 2nd place was not an option in my thinking. We memorized verses, sometimes whole chapters, most of which I remember to this day. Of course, everyone we knew, used only the King James Version.

My first model car was a prize from a Sunday School teacher, for Scripture memorization. I put together model cars, and model animal scenes up through junior high. At the end of the Sunday night service in church, there was a time for prayer.

Everyone prayed. It's just what we did. Most of the time I took this seriously. It was a time to ask for forgiveness and a time to make plans to do better in the future. Most of us know this was sometimes not as successful as planned.

An understanding of the Fear of the Lord, was developed. I didn't say a correct understanding, but nevertheless, an understanding took root. I would reset this definition more than once in life. The one thing I would say is, we thought it better to error on the side of caution, and refrain, than to throw caution to the wind and perish.

Yes, there was a lot of legalism in my upbringing. I tended to be an "It's clearly right or wrong," person, anyway. I would have my whole life to reassess and reevaluate all of these issues. The good thing is, I was given a framework that said, it is important to please God, to do what is right. Even with the pitfalls of teen living, in my heart, doing right, and pleasing God was what I wanted to do.

In the spirit of equal time, I know my kids, at least the older ones, would say I did the same thing as a parent. I was too strict. Part of this was due to church expectations, but not all of it.

A central part of the church's teaching was, God (Jesus) may, and probably will, come back at any time, to take the Christians to heaven. The term for this is the Rapture. It is not a term found in Scripture, but is used to summarize the overall great event in eschatology, the Christians leaving the earth to go to be with the Lord.

This brought continuous thought to, "Wherewithal shall a young man cleanse his way…(Psalm. 119:9, KJV of course)." Being "Left Behind" was the worst possible of circumstances.

I was considered a good kid. I was never in any trouble with the law, whether with the legal system of the courts, the church, or at home. I mostly chose to follow what was expected of me, curfew not withstanding.

The standards that were set and clearly defined kept me from making decisions in my youth that could have derailed or ruined my life. In today's terms, I would have been labeled as a compliant child, (mostly) rather than a defiant child, but in the fairness of equal time, I will tell you a little story.

In children's church, Sunday School, and even during Released Time (yes, on Wednesday mornings students were allowed to leave the public school system, walk to their churches, for a period of religious instruction), we would sing these little songs, like 'Climb, Climb Up Sunshine Mountain', 'I Met Jesus At The Crossroads', and 'If You're Saved and You Know It'. All of these songs had actions, or motions to them. I suppose you could call it hand choreography. I would not do the motions, even as a young grade schooler. I thought the motions were silly. I did not want to climb Sunshine Mountain. The usually gentle prodding of the Sunday School teachers fell on deaf ears. I just wouldn't do it.

As an important side note, this was a picture to the great dichotomy of my life. I always wanted to do it my way. I thought I knew a better way (You can ask my wife about some of my driving shortcuts.) And because my motives were pure, I thought everyone would see it my way.

Let's Go Camping

There was a church camp that the whole state went to. I was sometimes allowed to go for a week to kids camp and teen camps. The teen camps, especially, were a lot of fun. It was a mixture of church, activity, and looking for girls. My accomplishments in this area were about as good as my batting average. (More on that later.) On my Roy Orbison Greatest Hits CD, I think he gets the girl once or twice on the whole recording. It seems to be a universal percentage.

They also had, and still do, have a ten day camp for families. Some summers, my dad made it possible for us to stay there for a week, and he would join us on the weekend. Some of these times were very important in my spiritual development.

The rooms for after service prayer were segregated for the men and women. The sound of many men praying will always ring in my ears. It must have been very sweet to the heavens.

There was another great thing about camp, the summer I was fourteen. I met Dannie. A friend of mine knew a friend of his. We became acquainted and became best friends, to this day.

We lived out of state (out of Minnesota) during some of my kids' childhood, but they have all been to camp one time or another. In recent years I have been able to spend a couple days there each summer. It is still thriving. I was excited to see what seemed to be hundreds of kids bicycles. Families are still going to camp.

I did not see this coming...

Cut back to age eleven. I am sitting in church on a Sunday night, "minding my own business." The most shocking thing took place. To this day, it is the biggest surprise of my life. God placed a call on my life, for ministry. This stunned me, more than I could possibly imagine, much more than the Henry Ford marker. I mean, it's one thing to hear from Henry Ford. It's another thing to hear from God. There are lots of cars, and carmakers, but there is only one God.

I never expected this in a million years. I am sorry to tell you, in my own burning bush moment, the response of my heart was not nearly as good as Moses' response at the original burning bush (see Exodus 3). To my limited understanding, this meant becoming a pastor, a preacher. I had nothing against pastors. I think everyone loved our local pastor, but young as I was, I had already made a plan. Pulpit ministry was not a part of it.

To make matters worse, about a minute after God spoke to my heart, our pastor says, out loud, to the whole congregation, " God has called someone to ministry tonight." He wanted "that person" to come forward so they could pray with/for him. I froze. I did not respond. (In later years I told this story to that pastor.) Shortly after this he moved to a different town.

A family in the church had a vacant farm house. I think it was about 10 miles out of town. Instead of renting it out, it was turned into a Teen Center. Every other Thursday night it was a place for kids to meet. This included games, food, and a short church service. So many of the kids from the high school, and surrounding high schools were there at one time or another. This lasted for many years.

The sign that hung on the makeshift farmhouse pulpit read, "Remember now thy Creator in the days of thy youth." (Ecclesiastes 12:1 KJV) The sign did not include the second half of the verse, which reads, "while the evil days come not, nor the years draw nigh, when thou shalt say, I have no pleasure in them." (also KJV) As a teen, you never think the last half of the verse is possible.

CHAPTER FIVE | MY OWN PATH

I SOMEWHAT JOKINGLY TELL PEOPLE, including some co-workers, not to argue with we about four things, the music of my day, baseball, numbers, and the Bible.

The music started first. I remember as a very young child using the window sill as my pretend piano. We did not have a piano. One of the neighbors did. My aunt and uncle did. Grandpa Howard's youngest son lived a few miles from us. They had kids roughly our age. We grew up with these cousins. We still get to see them once in awhile.

I would go to these pianos and play them, as an early grade schooler. I knew nothing about music. I had been given zero lessons in my short life. I found out that I could sound out one finger melodies on these pianos. Eventually I graduated to two-finger-harmonies. I could play songs by ear, not well, or with any kind of flair (still true).

Set The Trumpet To Thy Mouth. Hosea 8:1 (KJV).

I'm in fifth grade. It's when students were able to begin taking free music lessons from the band director (grades five through twelve.) There were no instruments in our house. I previously had no idea, but my dad said he liked the violin and the tenor saxophone. Strings were not offered in school, and a new tenor saxophone at that time cost three hundred dollars. It might as well have been three million. What to do? We learned that a man in the church had an old silver cornet. My dad bought it for me for twenty-five dollars. To our family, that was still a lot of money.

Hold Your Horses

Another story of my life–slowdown, take it easy, not so fast. Before the cornet was bought it was "hold your horses" time. A music aptitude test had been given to all of the fifth graders. It was a 40 question test. I don't remember anything about the questions on the test. It was administered by the school's new band director, Bruce Pearson. (Yes, that Bruce Pearson.) He was straight out of college, in his first teaching assignment, probably 22 years old, with a newly minted B. A. He ended up in Verndale.

Fast forward for a moment. I'm an adult. We are living out of state. There's a family in our church. They have been friends for many years. They have a son who is struggling with his trombone. He wants to quit. They want me to see if I can help him. I go out to the house. On their piano sits a music instruction book, *Trombone for Beginners*, by Dr. Bruce Pearson. As a ten year old fifth grader, who knew?

I tell people I was his first student, when in fact, the whole fifth grade class qualifies for that distinct title. It's still not time to let the horses out of the gate. There is a problem with the test. OK. Not a problem with the test, but a problem with me. I failed the test, miserably. I wasn't even close. Even though I knew there was some raw, natural talent in me, this was a, "There's no hope for him," moment.

There is an open house at the school. The school owns some instruments, and the local music store from Wadena sent a representative out with some instrument for the future virtuosos to try, and hopefully, buy. They tell me my embouchure looks adaptable to several possibilities. A big chance is taken. A sacrifice is made. I get the cornet.

It turned out to be one of the best things that ever happened to me. For the most part, if anyone thought well of me, or thought I had any talent, it was because of the trumpet.

On about my second or third lesson I ask the future Dr. Pearson about some notations I see toward the back of the book. He feigns (I think) indignity. He tells me to not get ahead of myself, to slowdown, to learn the rudimentary stuff well, before I try other things. I had heard this message before, in other areas.

I am learning to read music. I am practicing. Boy am I ever practicing. An hour a day, or even two hours, was not unusual. It was not because I had to. I wanted to. I was my own motivation. (I've pretty much held to that).

We are still in the small green house. Sometimes I get sent out to the field, or to an old car on the property, to practice. (Finding an old car on the property was not a problem. It's a true story, but hard to believe. More on that later.) After just a few weeks I can play any song I know, without music, whether it's an old hymn from the church, or a song off the radio. I can hear it in my head and transfer it to the valves on the cornet. I had nothing to do with this. It was just a gift, something that was in me at birth. Discovering the talents, or gifts, God puts in us, and developing them is a whole 'nother book.

Our church has anyone play their instrument during the singing of the Sunday night service. I know I can do this, so I join the others. One of the young men from the church has grown up, gone to college, and is now a band director in another town. He just happens to be home for the weekend of my first time playing. He comes up to me before church starts, and sees I have only the church song book in front of me. He asks me if I know how to transpose. I have no idea what that means. (I'm only ten years old, maybe just turned eleven.) He tells me that the piano is keyed in C. My instrument is in B Flat. If I play notes from the same book the piano uses, I will be off by a note. I need to play everything a note higher, and add two sharps to each key signature. He saved me a monstrous embarrassment.

I took a church book home. I understood what he said. In a few weeks I am all set. I join what we call the church orchestra. It was usually a piano, a couple of accordions, and a guitar. Einer would join later, on trumpet, Scott on trombone or guitar.

The practicing pays off. By the end of fifth grade I am in my high school concert band. I get to leave class to go to band. I was so sad to have to miss diagraming sentences, or something like that. Actually my fifth grade teacher was probably my favorite teacher of all time. She knew more than what day of the week it was. She was extremely nice. She knew how to make learning an enjoyable experience.

Take Me Out To The Ball Game

When I was in first or second grade we got our first TV. It worked some of the time. When it didn't it was because mom was sure God did not want us to watch the available programming....*Leave it to Beaver* and *Superman* are two possibilities I remember.

Anyway, once in awhile a Minnesota Twins game would be on. I took no special notice.

The summer I was ten years old, there was a transformation. I found myself listening to the Twins on the radio. I was hooked. For life. I don't know why, or what it was about it that attracted me. Sometimes I will just as soon listen to a game on the radio as watch one on TV. I still enjoy sitting out on my deck with a cup of coffee or a ginger ale, maybe a snack or two, on a summer evening, and listening to a Twins game.

As a young teenager I got to go to my first Twins game. It was to help keep track of a group of younger kids. A monster was created, not the kids, but me.

My daughter Sara went to at least a dozen games before she was fifteen months old. For her sixteenth birthday, she asked me to take her to a baseball game. I at least did something right. My boys would go once in awhile. My wife has become more interested through the years due to my obsession. I can tell anyone far more than they would ever want to know, about baseball history, and statistics.

The old Metrodome (in downtown Minneapolis) was a wretched place, but general admission was about seven bucks. Sometimes you could sit in the family section and get a ticket, a hot dog, and a Coke for about twelve dollars. The good thing about the place was, you never had a rain out. I saw a lot of ballgames there.

The new Twins stadium, Target Field, 2010 model, is a great place for baseball. They did it right. It almost qualifies as a temple.

When I was in college, I got my dad to go to a baseball game with me at the old Metropolitan Stadium in

Bloomington. (Now home to the Mall Of America). I think him going to the baseball game was equal to my going to the rodeo. I had most likely bribed him in to going, with the plan to go to a Mr. Steak Restaurant, afterwards.

Timing is everything. As an adult, we moved out of state in early 1987, before the Twins won the 1987 World Series. We moved back to Minnesota in 1992, just after they won the 1991 World Series. I missed them both. The saving grace was, we missed the infamous Halloween blizzard of 1991.

Genesis, Exodus, Leviticus, Numbers

I like numbers. Numbers, and statistics are always going on in my head. That may be what drew me to baseball, and may be what helped me continue to do math in my head. Baseball has always been analyzed to the 'nth degree. Statistics go on and on. Now with analytics, even more so.

I'm in fourth grade. I think we are learning what was then called the new math. It's the same teacher from the days of the week. I turn in a long division math paper, (three or four numbers divided by two numbers). There is no work shown on it, just answers. She is not pleased. She wanted me to show my work. She wanted to know where I got the answers. I told her the answers came from my head. I can do them in my head. Why would I want to go to all of the trouble to write down a bunch of unnecessary figures? I offered to demonstrate. She was not amused.

One day during outside recess, (same teacher, same year) she decides that the best use of our most valuable time of the day should be spent doing the hokey pokey. I just could not bring myself to participate. Really, I did not participate.

Decades later, my wife and I are vacationing in the Florida Keys. I see a tee shirt in a shop window that asks the question, "What if it really is all about the Hokey Pokey?" I laughed out loud.

In those days, there was only one class per grade in the school. There was no way she (the fourth grade teacher) was not going to promote me at the end of the school year. She would have refused to have me for another year.

I like the statistics of baseball. I've done some floor covering sales work in the past. I enjoyed figuring the square footage and drawing the scale diagrams. I enjoyed irritating my boss by telling him the totals before he could come up with them on his calculator. The real math did not come as easily to me.

I took all of the high school math courses, with some A's and B's, but sometimes every day was a struggle, learning new things, especially in Geometry.

My son Elijah used the University of Minnesota freshman calculus textbook for his high school senior year of math. I told him, I was good in math, but not that good.

Uncle Bob

Uncle Bob was our high school math teacher. His name was Mr. Shultz. He was a no nonsense guy, but not in a bad way. He came complete with a crew cut, glasses, and always, always, white socks. We never referred to him in person as Uncle Bob. I don't think the "Uncle Bob" moniker started out as a term of endearment, but by the time we were through senior high, it was.

He had a way of reaching lost souls and giving them hope and helping them figure it out. I was not yet a lost soul, and he was determined to keep it that way.

One of the things in fashion in those days was to wear your shirt untucked. The shirt tails were very long, none of this squared off stuff like today. I suppose the untucked tails gave an unkempt, disheveled appearance. You were not allowed to cross the threshold of the door of the math department with an untucked shirt. He was serious. And compromise was not a word in his dictionary.

It was the end of my sophomore year, the difficult Geometry class, in particular. We had been required to keep a journal of all of the geometric theorems, and other data. At the end of the year Mr. Shultz wanted to know if this had any value. I offered that it did, because if he had not made us do it, I probably would not have done it.

Mr. Shultz was indignant. He did not feign anything. He challenged me on the spot, publicly. "Is that how you are going to go through life, doing only what is required? Are you only going to do what people make you do? Is that the only effort you are going to put forth?" Obviously, I never forgot that.

On the day I met Henry Ford (so to speak) that is how I was living. I was working hard. That's never been a problem. But the fight had been taken out of me. I was sad, angry, and did not have enough vision, hope, or energy to do anything about it. I was not sure there was anything that could be done.

At the end of our senior year it was time to sign yearbooks. Mr. Shultz signed our yearbooks, "Uncle Bob."

I really don't think he ever heard anyone refer to him as Uncle Bob. We think our English teacher did. The two were our senior class advisors. We think he told Mr. Shultz about his new title. Who knows? Neither teachers or parents are ever as dumb as kids think they are.

The English teacher was something else, on a variety of levels. I don't know if we ever knew if he knew a split infinitive from a dangling participle, (not that I would either) but long before we graduated, we knew how to do a term paper. He also gave me an appreciation for literature. I'm guessing that not everything on his reading syllabus would qualify as literature.

It's not on my list at the top of this chapter, but I love newspapers. The neighbor that had the piano also had the daily newspaper, from Minneapolis no less. I would read it when we would go over there. The lady was my mom's best friend, They, like us had seven kids. This was not as uncommon as one might think.

By the time I was in seventh grade, I would try to find time to get to the school library every day to read the Minneapolis paper. A cup of coffee and a newspaper are two of God's great gifts to mankind. My brother Einer is possibly the world's greatest all time coffee drinker. Daughter Sara loves coffee. My grandpa Fred used to let us drink coffee when we came to see him. (He never offered to share his chewing tobacco with us.) My brother Scott and I used to meet early in the morning for coffee on weekends.

My wife is one hundred percent Norwegian. (Our poor kids are mutts.) It's like the Norwegians invented coffee. They have coffee for breakfast at 6:00 AM, coffee with a treat at 9:00 AM, coffee for lunch, coffee with a snack/

treat mid-after noon, coffee for dinner, and late night coffee with a piece of pie before day's end.

A young lady once brought a book to church. The title was, 'First We Have Coffee'. I said to her. "I'm sure that was written by a Norwegian." Sure enough it was.

My most important time with coffee, ever, was the time I spent with Jonathan, for
hours on end.

CHAPTER SIX | CAN'T GROW UP FAST ENOUGH

HOME LIFE WAS COMPLICATED. When dad was home, sometimes he and mom would verbally spar (that's the polite term) in front of us kids. It was very unsettling. Only once was I afraid, literally, that it might turn in to something more than verbal. It did not.

All my dad did was work, a lot, and sleep, very little. When he was home, there were the farm things to take care of that us boys had not done, or did not know how to do. One time, during the week, we repaired the gate at the end of the fence. We tied it together with twine.

His response was, "You can't build a farm with twine string." We still use that phrase today to address mismanaged fixes. Chasing horses that have escaped the fence is a tough way to make a living.

One day we were sawing a very large log with a Swede saw. (All of us were required to be present wherever dad was, during the weekend farm escapades.) Einer is the third of the four boys. He has always had a very great sense of humor.Some would call it witty, sarcastic, cynical, or dry, but it is always hilarious.

He was trying to hold this log still, while Steve and dad did the sawing. Einer's efforts were not satisfactory, and dad told him so. Einer's response was, "Why don't you sit on it, maybe that will help."

The thin boxer was long gone. My guess is that dad went through most of his adult life at about two hundred and thirty to two hundred and forty pounds. He was twice as broad across the shoulders as I was. We thought Einer's life was over. Dad never said a word.

As a young teen I made the accurate assessment of my place (or lack of it) in my dad's life. There were times where I was angry at him, but I did not go through life thinking, I hate my dad. But I also knew, I did not want to be like him. He was angry.

I did not like the farm, the horses, the boxing.... I just kew that I viewed life a whole lot different than he did. I knew that he thought I would never "make it." It seemed that I was never able to please him. His work schedule did not allow him to see our sports games.The comments after the one junior basketball game and one senior high football game he was able to see, were not exactly encouraging. He did not understand my obsession with the music industry.

I received two compliments in my adult life from him. The one really was a compliment, but also included (by default) the fact that he had no expectation of me being able to accomplish anything.

The life and the relationship he had wanted was a combination of never was, and never would be again. I was able to articulate this to myself. I never talked to him about it. He was a man of few words. That was not uncommon for his generation.

Early in my college career, dad and I were both in Minneapolis on a summer weekend. The two of us went to Como Zoo. It was a nice day. (I don't mean weather-wise.) I was surprised.

The family used to go to the zoo when we kids were little. In fact one of my sisters was told that's where she came from. My dad had his own sense of humor. It did not always have universal acceptance.

He used to escape work, and slip away to the Upper Midwest Golden Gloves Boxing Tournaments in Minneapolis. A couple of times I joined him.

When I told him I was getting married, it was just the two of us at Mr. Steak. He didn't think that was a good idea (for him, the partial truth in humor), and not because he didn't like the young lady. He asked me if it was anybody he knew.

He was a very generous man. This did not fit with what we knew of the rest of his demeanor and communication, but he was. Christmas was great, complete with last minute wrapping. I can't overstate how hard he worked to provide for the family.

As far as we knew, no one in our circle of acquaintances had any money. No one was fashion conscious, (except Uncle Bob). I did not think of us as poor, but we knew money was tight enough and not to be wasted.

When we were little, he took us to see the Shrine Circus in Minneapolis, several times. Once I decided that I wanted to be a circus trumpeter. They played with a live orchestra/band.

Even after moving back to the farm after third grade, we still found ourselves in Minneapolis on occasion. It was a privilege a lot of our friends did not have.

While we lived north of the metro, dad took us boys with him to see what we now would call the WWE. I was actually scared some of the time. It did not look fake to a kid of my age.

Dad loved to shop, but only for bargains. Later in life, before he retired, he was living in the cities (combo name throughout the Midwest for Minneapolis and St. Paul).

He amassed enough "stuff" to fill five different storage facilities in five different places. He bought a trailer and hauled all the stuff up to the farm when he moved back there after retirement.

I mentioned the cars. Dad bought cheap cars, and ran them until they died, which might be a week or a year. Sometimes he bought cars that did not run at all, to use for parts for cars he hoped to keep running. Sometimes he bought cars with real value, that did not run, or run right, with the idea of fixing them. None of it ever happened.

I have, more than once, in the middle the night, sat in a cold car and steered, while it was being towed, with only a chain, the one hundred and fifty miles from Minneapolis to the farm. It was not acceptable to break a headlight, while turning a corner, on the car being towed. I'd like to say it never happened.

I learned to drive in an old, very old 1949 International pickup. The shift protruded from the floor. It seemed about six feet long, and had lots of play in it. Automobile driving was never "new" to farm kids. Everyone drove tractor, probably long before they should have.

The good thing about all of this, was that there was usually a car around that ran that we could use. Dad wanted us to play sports. We were able to get to the school and back to catch the bus for games. (My dad's track practice consisted of him running home from school because his dad couldn't (or wouldn't) pick him up.

When my dad sold the farm there were two hundred–that's not a misprint–two hundred non-running vehicles on the property, plus a few that ran. He moved a few of the ones he still valued off site. The rest he had crushed for scrap metal.

I still regret that I did not have the money to buy the farm, or least ten acres, out by the road. I had enough chaos in my life, without being an absentee owner. I once, non-seriously suggested we move to Verndale. Son Elijah said, "Have fun dad, I'll write."

Years later, before he bought a house in Deer Creek, dad was living in a mobile home behind a walled fence on a friend's property. He had amassed another one hundred cars.

For years, he wintered in Truth or Consequences, New Mexico. My youngest brother Scott has been down there. I never did ask him about the southern car count. Dad's eightieth birthday was titled, "Eighty Years of Cars."

Gentlemen, Start Your Engines...

In the spring of my junior year dad made the unfathomable, out of character purchase. He bought a brand new car. True to form, he shopped, and found a great bargain. It was a year and a half old by now, but had never been sold, so it still was brand new. What's more, it was a four speed, very stylish. Some weeks it was with him in the cities. some weeks it was home for us boys to use. Through the years, I was the only son to never put a scratch on that car.

When we were young, dad sometimes talked about moving to Oregon. His only brother, Luther, lived in Portland. Dad visited him after high school. Luther was always known as Bud. My dad was never able to pull the trigger on the idea of the move. Years later, I would understand that very well. Moves to Louisville and Seattle were very seriously considered, talked about, even planned, especially Louisville, but I couldn't do it.

CHAPTER SEVEN | TEEN LIGHTS (Highs and Lows)

The Music

LIFE WAS VERY BUSY, VERY FULL. There was football in the fall, basketball in the winter, and track in the spring. There was band, and choir, the school yearbook staff, and student council.

My trumpet, (the cornet had to be put to rest) was silver, nice, and a school owned instrument. I guarded it with my life. It had become the love of my life. If I would have had to choose between music or sports, it would have been a tough decision (I'm not telling). I had become first chair at the beginning of my freshman year. The future Dr. Pearson was long gone. He only stayed two years.

During my sophomore year Dr. Pearson brought his award winning high school band to our school for a concert. They blew me away.

During the summer of going into eighth grade, Mr. Masog, came to town to be the band director. I think his personal band instrument had been the clarinet. It also happened that he was a classically trained, virtuoso, piano player. This proved invaluable to me.

Every year there was a solo and ensemble music contest. A performance piece

as practiced, hopefully to perfection. If the judge at the district level gave you an A, you were allowed to go the the state contest. Almost all of the solo performances were accompanied by a piano. Mr. Masog was flawless. I participated every year.

Glory Days - (Bruce Springsteen)
(Well at least some of the time)

In eighth grade I had already played my contest piece at the state "music meet." I heard another trumpeter play a piece, by memory, at this contest. I had no idea what it was. It was beautiful, and extremely difficult. When it came time to select my choice of music for next year's competition, I was trying to explain the composition I had heard to Mr. Masog. He had an idea. He produced a copy of Haydn's Concerto for Trumpet. That was the one. I think Mr. Masog was a little skeptical. The concerto was beyond my ability. It didn't matter. I attacked the third movement with reckless abandon.

For the district contest I played better than any previous attempt. I surprised myself. The kind judge asked me, "How old are you?" I told him, fifteen. He smiled. When the judge's scores were posted, I had squeaked by with an A- next to my name. I was thrilled, and on to the state contest. Later we were given the judge's written remarks. Along with his comments on my performance, both good and, could be better, he praised Mr. Masog for his superb accompaniment.

Not every performance is a great memory. Such was the state contest the following spring. It was time for an encore for Mr. Hayden. When I got to the room where I would play, I had a surprise. "Tom" was the young man scheduled to play right before me. He was a senior from another town. I had met him at church camp
many years before. He was already a renowned musician, on baritone and trombone. I'm sure he would have been first chair at the college of his choice, any college.

Me, playing after him, was like putting the drawing of a stick man next to a Rembrandt.

Tom's performance was properly acknowledged, appreciated, and applauded. Mine, less so. I did not do that well. Again, the judge, (a different one,) asked me how old I was. His short verbal comments amounted to, basically, "Keep your head up, you have lots of years ahead of you." I did not need to wait for the ratings to be posted or for the judge's written comments to know there would be no A.

The next year, I chose a piece that I had total confidence in, memorized it, and nailed it at both district and state. Redemption was sweet.

I was scheduled to play at a school awards banquet. I told Mr. Masog I wanted to play Mac Arthur Park, the one of a kind song written by Jimmy Webb and performed by Richard Harris. He was able to find a copy of the sheet music.

Mr. Masog was unfamiliar with the song. This gifted musician was not sure what to do with it, or exactly how the intricate rhythms should be played. I gave him my recording of the song. The performance went very well. it was a lot of fun. The applause was as much for Mr. Masog's perfect rendition of the long interlude, as it was for the trumpet. To this day it is one of my favorite memories of young life.

Seeing Jimmy Webb in concert at a small, somewhat intimate venue, with just him, a piano, his music, and his stories, was a highlight of more recent life, as was the chance meeting after the concert.

I did not revisit Haydn again until my senior year, playing the first movement of that concerto. You know, that high E flat was just never a guarantee.

The Great One…

There was only one television station available for farm TVs in Verndale. I don't think it was NBC. Anyway, if I was ever caught watching the Tonight Show with host Jonny Carson, it would have been the end. Needless to say, we all knew of Doc Severinsen, the musical director, and most renowned trumpeter of his day. (With apologies to Al Hirt.)

I'm well aware that many of you reading this book have never heard of many of the musicians and songs that are referenced. I have a lengthy music library. Just the trumpeters include Doc Severinsen, Al Hirt, Herb Alpert, Miles Davis, Wynton Marsalis, Chris Botti, and Phil Driscoll. I need to include Louie Armstrong, Maynard Ferguson, and Dizzy Gillespie.

Some things are impossible to forget. It is almost impossible to express enough gratitude for the following story: One winter night, Mr. Masog took some of us to St. Cloud St. University. On the way, I think we had pizza and spumoni ice cream for dinner. Hey, we were teenagers. Mr. Masog had tickets. Tickets to what, you ask? He took us to see Doc Severinsen. Bad weather delayed his plane. The show started very late. Doc gave a complete, mesmerizing performance. So kids, keep practicing your trumpets and pianos.

Mr. Masog retired from Verndale High School. It is a great treat to get to see him on occasion when I am able to return "home." They rightfully named the high school auditorium in his name.

I can still remember all of the music to all of my contest pieces, and probably half of the music we played in band.

My brother Einer played the baritone, Scott the trombone. My sister Melody, the clarinet, sister Dawn the trumpet. I borrowed all of their instruments, and learned to play them somewhat. My dad had picked up an old silver C Melody saxophone at a garage sale. I really enjoyed that. Brother Steve was a drummer. I made no attempt, (no rhythm).

I began doing music trumpet arrangements, mostly of church music. I got to play them for various functions.

I made some attempt at original music. I still have some copies of some of my old lyrics, which now make virtually no sense whatsoever.

Two Barbarians Storm the Gate

Christmas was especially good when I was sixteen. All of a sudden, the trumpet had competition, real competition. My dad got me an electric guitar with a small amp. Most of the time I had to leave the amp off. The electric guitar did not translate to going outside someplace to practice.

I also soon had an acoustic guitar. I taught myself chord structure and became a self taught guitar player. I played for hours and hours and hours on end. The trumpet and guitar would help open a lot of doors for me in years to come. Another love of my life was added to my growing list.

Somewhere in my late teen years an old piano ended up on our porch. I was determined I would to be able to play piano by the time I got out of high school. I could read music for the trumpet, or guitar, but never having piano lessons, I learned to play strictly by ear, using the chord knowledge I learned from the guitar.

For a number of years, I was the piano player for a church, more out of necessity than sheer talent. That took a lot of practice time. I still play piano, mostly to write music, and for my own enjoyment. I would say I play a composer's piano, rather than a performance piano. But it is another love of my life.

As a senior, I tried out for All State Band. I heard an audition by a trumpeter from Brainerd. Wow! By the time I heard a trumpeter from Wadena play The Carnival of Venice for his audition, I knew my chances were null and void. The consolation, was, before the end that year, we beat Wadena in basketball and track.

Years later, I have a niece, who plays the flute. She makes the All State Band, as a sophomore. How my brother got such talented and brilliant kids is a mystery.

Baseball

There was no baseball. Can you believe it? I can't play baseball. I can run. I can catch, sometimes. But I can't throw. I could do a hundred plus push ups, but I can't throw a baseball. I can throw a football, almost as far as I can throw a baseball. I learned all of this the summer I was thirteen or fourteen. I played a summer of Babe Ruth League Baseball.

The later to be named "Uncle Bob" was the coach. My bating average was .143. I found out I was not that fond of having another teenager standing sixty and one half feet away, (even if he was a friend), and neither one of us was exactly sure where that pitch was going.

A .143 average is not going to attract any scouts, only calls from the the grandstand, not positive ones. Local sports fans were always very vocal. I did learn how to properly score a baseball game in the book. My baseball career was limited to cheering for the Twins.

A note from childhood. My dad was a very good baseball player. He tried to teach us. Many Sunday afternoons were spent at a very nice, large park in Wadena. After a picnic lunch we would go to the baseball field to play workup, a version of baseball with limited players.

My brother Steve and I were digging a hole. We were probably 4 and 5. We got the shovel far enough in to the ground to have it stand up straight. We could not get any deeper. We made a regretful decision. We each got one of dad's baseball bats and pounded on the metal part of the shovel, on each side of the handle. The bats were badly dented. I honestly can't remember if we became badly dented or not.

One day my wife and I discovered our twins, about two years old, had inexplicably taken snow shovels to the hood of one of our cars, the one that was given to us by the in-laws. The twins were cute, and loved by the in-laws, but this was impossible to explain.

Instead of baseball, I turned to all the other available sports. I could run. I qualified for a track letter in eighth grade by placing for a ribbon on the high school mile relay team. (They were desperate). We had a great track coach. I also had a great half mile run that year. The coach thought I could progress and go to the state meet later in senior high. It was his last year.

My freshman track year was a disaster. I had some leg injury. I weighed eight pounds more than I would as a senior in track. I wondered if there was any future in it.

The fall of my sophomore year we got a new football coach, Mr. Mahlen. Once again, someone straight out of college. He was enthusiastic, seemed to relate to us, and seemed to definitely know what he was doing. (Since we were so qualified to make that analysis.) I was never a great football player, but I was the starting left end as a sophomore.

Mr Mahlen was also the the Phy. Ed. teacher. On the morning of our last game of the season, the grass was a little wet for Phy. Ed. We had been playing soccer. He told us to play touch football so no one would get hurt or worn out. I broke my collar bone.

Oh, by the way, Mr. Mahlen is still there, coaching football. He is in the Minnesota High School Hall Of Fame. It is a close, three way contest, but he also is the all time winningest coach in the entire state of Minnesota, in any division. The Verndale field is properly named Mahlen Field, in perpetuity,

It was my opinion that he was a better track coach than football coach. He resurrected my track career and our program. Track is grueling, especially the 440 yard dash. (We ran in yards, not meters back in those ancient times.)

One of my favorite track moments came against Sebeka, an arch rival in all sports. I anchored the mile relay team. (I think all of our times were equal.) I got the baton a step and a half ahead of my competitor. I could hear him the entire time, all the way around the track, but I never saw him.

We had great success as a team. I think my friend Mark tied the school record in the hundred yard dash. I think one of our relay teams made it to state. I did not.

Our take on the Wadena miler was that he couldn't break sixty seconds in the quarter mile, but that he could run four sixty second laps in a row.. That was my race. I had no chance.

Our basketball coach came to town when I was a sophomore. He was great. I made the varsity as a junior, barely. I wasn't that good. I could run. I could shoot. Defense was another issue, and I can't jump. I did however, win the laps in practice. It may be more truth than humor, but I tell people, that's why he let me on the team. I think we lost one conference game in a four year stretch, (to Sebeka of course.)

We did not have anyone over six feet tall. Our goal was to run teams off the court, and we did. Every change of possession was to be seen as a potential fast break, rebound, outlet pass, downcourt, and shoot. Take good shots, but shoot. We averaged eighty-two points a game my junior year.

I think we scored one hundred points three times that year. That just didn't happen in those days. One game was so lopsided, I was on the floor at the beginning of the second quarter. Later in the game I missed a free throw that would have been the one hundredth point. We won 114-47.

In one game the opposing coach had to be coaxed to leave his team on the floor to complete the game. It was 90-30 after three quarters.

One year, when Menagha came to town for a conference game, we won 74-44. We returned to Menagha later in the season for the rematch. They stalled the entire game. They did not panic. They only shot if they could find an open layup. The Verndale fans were livid.

Our coach did not panic either. He told the team how to respond. The outcome was not decided until late in the game. We won 15-12. I give that opposing coach a lot of credit. He had a plan.

My senior year we had beaten Aitken, a much larger school in a different conference. In the District Sectional Tournament, Aitken was way ahead of the tourney favorite, Crosby Ironton. The games were being played at Brainerd High School. Some old guy (he was probably 45?) stands up in the crowd, and by himself, starts yelling , "Go C I, Go, Go, C I, Go." We wanted him to sit down and shut up. We knew we could beat Aitken.

Soon he had half of the stadium on their feet, yelling Go, C I, Go, etc. And they did. It was an incredible display, not only by the winning team, but about what a difference one person with enthusiasm can make.

We were in the finals of that tournament against "C I." We were in the game at the very end, but lost. They had to go through Verndale on the next leg of the journey to the state tournament. In the spirit of sportsmanship, we hung banners by the Verndale sign on the edge of town that read: GO C I Go. And they did.

Minnesota only had one division in basketball at that time, so making the state tournament was a really big deal. In the state tournament, Crosby Ironton took the eventual state champs to overtime, and ended up in third place. We were that close.

Bible

There was no way to escape the age eleven church service. It was on my mind, heavily, every day of my life. I still couldn't believe it. I could not possibly imagine why this had happened. And I still was not happy about it. I told absolutely no one. It was a very real struggle for my conscience. How do you say no to God? That is what I wanted to do, and that is where I lived, in turmoil, for years.

Water Baptism was (and is) of great emphasis by the church. I had never been baptized. We are talking immersion, like in a river, or a lake. I was way too old to not be baptized. I wanted to wait, until I knew that being a Christian was what I really wanted to do. By the time I was fourteen, I had made a decision. I would be a Christian, forever. I would work out "the question" with God as time went along. I was baptized in the Crow Wing River.

There was no critical moment, no sudden impulse, no flashing lights, or dynamic enlightenment that caused me to forever alter the course of my life. That is how many of my long term, important life decisions have been made. They have evolved over time, through thought, and prayer, rather than sudden impulse. A lot of my sudden impulses never take place.

This was the first time I developed the thought, (at least for me) of being willing to be willing. That's not so much of a yes, as it is, "*If You can make it happen, let's* see what happens."

Slowing, and gradually, the chasm between the concept of ministry, and my life, began to narrow. Our grade school, junior and senior high school were all in one big (OK, not that big) building. I was talking to Mrs. Hopp, my former fifth grade teacher. She asked what I was going to do after high school graduation, which was not that far away. I told her I thought I was going to be a minister. She thought that was fine. She was so nice.I think this was my first verbal acknowledgement.

Hold on to sixteen as long as you can…John Mellancamp

Sixteen had come and gone. Life was about to get serious. The days of carefree living were about to be gone. Okay - I was never misinterpreted as a throw caution to the wind, carefree guy. Decisions had to be made.

I had a girlfriend. This one had lasted the better part of a year and a half. The thing was, I don't know if there was a better part to it. It was never the happiest of relationships, which was my fault. I did not deserve her. I should have treated her better.

During the last half of my senior year I answered my own question. Did I want to spend the rest of my life with her? I had no real reason to say no, but I told myself, no. We had not seriously discussed marriage, but we knew it was a possibility.

During the break up I did not play the bad guy. I was the bad guy. I did not handle it well. I did not do or say the right things.

Years later I met her and her husband at a summer, town celebration. I later told my wife, that when I left that conversation, I was sure she told her husband, "Thank God, I didn't marry him." I don't think she referred to me as the one that got away.

CHAPTER EIGHT |WHEN I FALL IN LOVE

I ALREADY LOVED MINNEAPOLIS. As an adult, I have now moved away, and come back, three times, four, if you count an internship. In the past, my wife has said, she doesn't think I will ever leave again.

As I already have said, my only concept of ministry, was pastoral. There is a
college, in fact several, in Minneapolis where you can get a four year education, with this as your goal. You will be qualified, at least on paper.

I got a great job in Minneapolis right out of high school. It was so good that I thought I might work a year, save a lot of money, and go to school somewhere where it was warm. Almost as an afterthought I sent my application in to a Minneapolis school, got enrolled, and started classes in the fall.

My job had gone so well, they started a second shift, for three days a week, and made me the supervisor, complete with a thirty-three percent raise. I had worked very hard, not missed a day, and I don't think I was ever late.

The high school grades had come easy enough. That, and my extra curricular activities, allowed me to be in the National Honor Society for two years in high school. I was under no illusion that college would be as easy. I was right. I had no idea what to expect. I had never discussed college life with anyone.

I knew my dad would not be able to put any of us through school. At one time, after I graduated, all six of my siblings were in college somewhere, at the same time. That would have been one huge bill.

I made a decision to work hard, study hard, and not to date. I did work hard. I took everything seriously. I paid my way through a private school and got out debt free. Tuition costs have skyrocketed in comparison to wages since then, making that nearly impossible today.

There were times where I slept two hours in the afternoon, and two hours at night, in between classes, work, and study.

I studied hard. It was a struggle just to get a 3.0 the first two years. I eventually upped my performance during the last two years, including one 4.0. I'm sorry, but I really was proud of that.

Is There A Musician In The House?

There were auditions for the college band. A seriously gifted director came to chair the music department the fall of my freshman year. I did not have time for choir, (or band for that matter either,) but here I am, in college band.

I think I had one date that fall. We double dated with friends and went, where else, to the Shrine Circus. It was just a friendship date. Besides, she was a better trumpet player than me.

A clarinet player was at the school. He had played first chair at two large universities, and had traveled in an all star international youth orchestra that was conducted by Leonard Bernstein. I heard that a young lady came to school after the end of first semester, and actually performed better than the star, in her audition. I don't know if we were ever formally introduced, but she seemed like a nice enough young lady.

On the Road Again... Willie Nelson

It's late spring, freshman year. The band is on tour. We were just south of Cheyenne, Wyoming, on our way to the Denver, Colorado area. There is going to be enough time in the schedule for us to do some mountain climbing.

I am sitting on the bus, "just minding my own business." Life as I know it is about to take a momentous turn. It was the unexpected, out of nowhere experience. Several rows of seats in front of me is the second semester clarinet player.

I am smitten. I might just as well have been hit by lightning. All of a sudden my eyes were opened. I start talking to myself. "Brian, where have you been? What have you been thinking? You better start paying attention." Due to previous experience, comes the question "Do I have a shot? Is there even any chance?"

I did not necessarily believe in falling in love. I didn't know if I was in love. But I liked whatever anyone wanted to call it. This whole idea of not dating did not seem like such a good idea anymore.

She didn't climb the whole four thousand foot mountain peak, but four of us did. I didn't climb, I flew. I had never felt like this, ever. By evening some kind of a connection had been made. I don't remember the details. I had lost my glasses, along with the rest of my head, and cold, hardened heart. One of my friends in the band told me she had found the glasses. He knew I had an interest.

I was not only completely gone, but I was scared. I had not done well in the last relationship. It was painful enough, that I knew I did not want to go through that again.

I only wanted one more relationship, a permanent one. I did not think it wise to be so presumptuous as to tell her that. So I made an attempt through this composition: It began:

Afraid to start, for fear it might end.
But what says my heart, says you are my friend.

Her name is Peggy. We had a few dates that spring. One was to a wedding. I played my trumpet in the balcony of a Catholic church for the pre-ceremony, and my guitar along with a female vocalist friend of the groom for the ceremony. It was my first Catholic service. Later that night we had a nice dinner at where else, Mr. Steak.

She went with me that spring when I went to pick up my first car. It was a Pontiac LeMans, five years old, with sixty thousand miles on it. I paid six hundred dollars cash. My, how times have changed.

That spring after extensive shopping, and sampling in practice rooms at multiple music stores, I bought a brand new trumpet, a silver Bach Stradivarius model. I also paid cash. I told you I worked hard. Three new loves in one spring was a veritable plethora of riches.

We had a few dates that spring before she went home for the summer to work, and before I buried myself in my more than one job, sixty hour plus work weeks, I had given her my address. Each of us had a few dates that summer with a long term high school friend. I did't hear from her. I called her. I had given her the wrong address. Some times ya just don't have a brain in your head.

She came through Minneapolis that summer with her parents and a brother. They were on there way to the West coast for a family vacation.

A side note: my family had never been on a vacation. I learned to water ski at my uncle and aunt's lake cabin in northwestern Wisconsin. We spent some holidays at their house in Duluth, and some holidays in Pillager, MN at another aunt and uncles'. The connection to both families, was, that they were my dad's sisters. We kids loved these trips. Einer was the name of the uncle from Duluth. His wife's name was Nita. We loved them, and they were great to us kids. Where else would my German/English brother get his Swedish name? Dad says we are German/English. Mom says we are English/ German.

The meeting with Peggy's parents went well enough, (I think.) We met downtown at the Embers Restaurant. It was open 24 hours a day. For years, I, and/or sometimes a brother would do the cleaning in this restaurant between four and six in the morning, anywhere from two to seven days a week.

I made arrangements to make the three hundred mile trip to pick up Peggy at the end of the summer and bring her back to school. And yes, during my first dinner at the Johnson family home, I spilled an entire glass of milk.

During a long talk at the end of the short driveway, we decide to make a go of it. It was tough for me to make the decision. Why? Because I wasn't being that bright. The brain cells were still having trouble making the right connection. She was patient. Once I made the commitment I was ecstatic. It wasn't a commitment marriage, just a commitment to go together.

I became the choir director of a metro church at the beginning of my sophomore year. We now had a church home. (Decades later my daughter would do work for a man who was the adult Sunday School teacher at that church. It is a small world.) We did a Christmas cantata that fall. It went well.

Our friends kept asking us when we were going to get engaged. In no more than four months I knew I wanted to spend the rest of my life with Peggy. The girl never did get a formal proposal. It was an awkward, left handed, stumbling, unprepared statement. I went home that night thinking, "Did I just ask her to marry me? " Not cool.

We've always said, one of the things we would do over again, is get married a year earlier. Graduation required a summer internship. I wanted to do that single. I did not think that heading to some place unknown, to face the unknown, with a brand new bride, seemed like a good idea. I took my internship after my sophomore year, a year earlier than normal.

We got formally engaged during the fall of my junior year. I had no money. The job I had lined up after internship was with a new company. It was not ready for start up. Actually, it was an offshoot of my first summer job. A salesman (Buddy) from that company was asked by our main customer to start his own company. I and the office manager were the only people he took with him. Once it got going it was great. It was one of my all-time favorite jobs. The company is still in operation. I live a mile and a half rom its operations center. Life has a way of coming full circle.

Our courtship/dating went extremely well. We literally had only one argument. It was significant, but didn't last as a long term issue. I started work in a fast food
estaurant. I then found a great paying job, beyond my wildest dreams. My (and soon, our) finances were looking good. She had a very good job working downtown.

We went to Duluth for a weekend. Uncle Einer had been the crazy, off the charts, off the wall, fun uncle. By the time Peggy met him he was in shambles. He and our favorite aunt were now divorced. He never fully recovered. He worked in the printing industry. He did our invitations as a wedding gift. We went to a University of Duluth hockey game.

Our premarital counseling was interesting, to say the least. One couple more or less told us that marriage was not that great, that we had a good chance to get along and do ok, but not to have any great expectations.

The wedding was held in Peggy's home church. It was a partly cloudy June day. The wedding was in the evening. Knowing my family, and fearing some of our friends, I had our car hid in the garage of a family from the church. I wanted a clean day, without any shenanigans.

The ceremony was officiated by Peggy's stately, well respected, long term pastor. Dannie, from camp, was best man, and two great friends, Steve and Glen were groomsmen. Peggy had three bridesmaids from college. The reception was downstairs in the very well appointed church basement.

My brother Scott sang some of the music. Groomsman Steve sang as we knelt at an altar and made two vows. We would walk with God, and with each other. The name of the song was “I’ll Walk With God.” Both vows were kept. Writing this brings good tears to my eyes.

CHAPTER NINE | FINAL PREPARATIONS

THIS SOUNDS LIKE WE ARE getting ready for a funeral. Don't laugh. There's always some truth to humor.The first year of marriage was also the last year of college. Oh, and by the way, during the fall of my junior year, I was not the only 4.0. Peggy was not to be left out. On The Dean's list, outside his office door, below my name, (only for alphabetical reasons) was Peggy's name. We had both pulled a 4.0 during the semester we got engaged. We did not have any classes together.

We had a great first year of marriage, beyond our expectations. I/we took life and studies seriously, but life was also fun, and good. We bought another car, only two years old. Life was looking good.

The spring of senior year is always tense. For some, they hope to find a mate, and don't. The main cause of concern is, where will I end up? Will I find placement? Most grads tried to find a position as an assistant pastor somewhere. Those were not easy to get. I immediately found out that there are always far more candidates, than open positions. This was not advertised in the glossy college brochures.

My internship had been with one of the organization's nationally renowned leaders. During that summer I also had the opportunity to be under another man who had a great national reputation. I knew this would not hurt my chances.

It's an incomplete science, trying to determine God's will. There are interviews, personalities, preferences, and yes, sometimes, politics. Not always, but way too often, it was hard to make distinctions, or be sure you made the right decision.

In the spring, organizational leaders from many surrounding states come to town to interview soon to be grads. I thought I had a very good interview with one of these men. I would come to have great respect for him. He would take a keen interest in my career. I would walk in to his state office one day, and there sits one of our bridesmaids, as his office manager.

Not long after our interview I received a letter from him. It listed five ministers in his state that were looking for assistants. I was free to contact any or all of them. Before I did, one of them contacted me.

I was on the final band tour. These were always great fun. This year I played baritone in the band, (a good, but long story,) a trumpet duet with our 1st trumpeter, (another musician with skills way beyond my ability) and played my guitar with my brother Scott during a vocal duet. He is the singer, not me. There is no question about that.

The trumpeter and I got to take turns as student conductors, much more than planned. The conductor suffered a severe leg injury playing basketball with us.

Word came to me in Huron, S.D. There was a phone call for me. I called back. It was one of the pastors on the list. He came to Minneapolis to interview us. He took us to lunch at the top of the IDS tower downtown. We agreed to move, far away. We were excited. This was really happening.

We sent our engagement picture on ahead, to the church. One of the young ladies in the church was quoted to us, saying, "She can't be that pretty."

During my last year I was the assistant choir director at the organization's most recognized church in the state. I ended up conducting for the Easter production. During one rehearsal, a young lady came to fill in for our regular pianist. She sight read everything, to perfection. I knew her cousins from early Verndale days. She also ended up being Mrs. Scott Borchers.

Peggy and I were invited to a Valentine's Day dinner party at the home of one of the families from the church. They asked me to sing a song as part of the event. I took a chance. I loved Al Martino's song, Mary In The Morning. I just adapted it to, *My Love In The Morning.* The song could have been considered a little risqué for a church crowd. However, this was a couple's event. And besides, the *young lady deserved the song.*

Before running away from home to our new adventure, we had two great events.We took our first vacation. It was just a long three day weekend, but we went to a nice resort in Alexandria.

I also got to be best man in groomsman Steve's wedding. For a couple of years, Steve and I met at a nice hotel for a school year end celebratory breakfast.

PART TWO

DOWN FOR THE COUNT

CHAPTER TEN: A ONE, TWO PUNCH

THESE WERE NOT PRACTICE PUNCHES, thrown in to the palms of an enthusiastic dad, but monstrous, thundering blows from unexpected corners. Again, this was totally unexpected. I was unprepared. That is a colossal understatement.

We gave our new church our housing budget. They would find a place for us to live. (Talk about going out on a limb.) They did, the day before we arrived. They spent that day and night painting. We had our moving truck, towing our Chevy Nova behind it. After three years, and thirty six thousand miles, I still got half of what I paid for the Pontiac. (Pontiac's long decline and eventual demise is a sad part of automobile history.)

We drove half way and stopped early. Peggy carried her flowers. It was our first anniversary. We had a good dinner and spent the night at a nice hotel. We did not realize it at the time, but we had been comparatively rich college students.

My new church responsibilities included the youth and music programs. I volunteered to help the bus ministry director. Later, when Sara was born, we thought of him (the bus director) as daughter Sara's unofficial godfather. Sara was born on his birthday. Sara's middle name is the same as his daughter's.

With my beginner's salary, Peggy needed to work. She was a highly skilled receptionist, administrative assistant. My taking a job that could not support both of us, put an unnecessary strain on us. We had not moved to a large city. She couldn't find a job. After months and months, we finally hired a recruiter. She found a very good job in a much larger city, nearby.

I had only been at our new assignment two months when my boss realized he made a mistake in hiring me. At the four month mark he wanted to send me back to Minneapolis. Our new life was nothing like we expected. Disillusionment was a mild term to describe our analysis, especially for Peggy. I had put us in financial trouble, and the strain in my professional relationship became equally matched by the strain that was developing at home.

The job was one punch. The almost totally stress free marriage, now wasn't. That was the second punch. A left jab and a right handed haymaker. Peggy had no outlet. There was no one for her to talk to.

I was at least, still standing. My attempt at ministry mirrored nothing of the stability she knew in her home church. I need to spare you all of the particulars of what happened. There were many instances that indicated I was either in the wrong place, or working for the wrong man.

Any thought that I was in the wrong field did not enter my mind. It would seem that surprises and disillusionment are not that foreign in any new career. This was deeper than the normal career jitters or job acclimation.

In hindsight, we would have moved back to Minneapolis at the four month mark to reassess. Instead, we were at this location about 18 months. Our teens had come in third place in a state contest. The music department did well. The bus ministry flourished. At the end of the year I got a good raise. But I knew I/we had to leave. I was devastated.

Two months after we left, the senior pastor left to go in to business. We met, years later, had good conversations. All was well.

A two-headed animal is called a monstrosity. There have been very, very few times in our marriage where I thought I needed to to be the final voice of a split decision. Going to our next assignment was such a case.

The church was a few years old. The senior pastor had started the church, fresh out of college. By the end of our first service there, we knew he was a young superstar. We knew he was headed to the "White House," someday. That was my term for the national headquarters. I use common terms to describe his ascent. It was also clear he was a man of God first, who also possessed a great charisma, great drive, and talent.

People did not come to church to see a show. They came, lots of them, because they knew they would hear something important that could help their lives.

As for ministry, my job, this was a worse fit than the first time around. I was working with a great man. Some specific assignments/expectations were really hard for me to accept. And finances were again an issue. We were there a very short time. A short tenure for an associate was actually (and sadly) not that unusual.

I had a good long talk with the "bishop" (state director) of the organization. This was the same man who came to the college to interview graduates.

He wasn't sure if it would be the right place for an inaugural voyage, but he let me know of a little church in a little town that needed a senior pastor. If accepted, I would no longer be an associate, I would be pastoring church. I was not overly confident, but neither was I scared.

The interview consisted of two questions. Would I mow the lawn, and could Peggy cook? They had a couple of acres of lawn, and loved their pot lucks. The answer to both questions was yes. We went ahead and conducted the rest of the interview.

The total church income for the previous year was less than what we had spent as a family, (Just the two of us.) There was no church or parsonage mortgage. It wasn't as bad as it sounded. I had to do something. If they were willing to take a chance on me, why not. It seemed to be the thing to do. Prayer was involved. Advice was sought.

We were once given the advice of, "You have go with what you've got." It was given as a means to discerning Divine guidance. That's what we did. We made decisions based on the best that we could do with the information and understanding we had.

And as for the money - It was considered a "normal" thing to be underpaid and you and God would figure out how to make it work. It was years later, we heard, "God can confirm his will as much by withholding money, as he can by providing it." In other words, if the money isn't there, don't go. How's that for controversy.

The state organization technically had oversight authority. I already knew I had their blessing. I left on good terms with my rock star boss. He did not have a Rock Star attitude, but everyone knew he was, and was going to be, very successful. (Yes, he made it to the "White House.")

We were approved, receiving a "yea" with all of the votes cast, save one.

They gave me a nice raise over what the previous pastor received, with the promise of more to come as the finances increased. Life was still a struggle for Peggy and me. On top of this there was some health trouble for her.

She was (is) the sweetest, kindest most gracious person on the planet. My bad choices would bring continued financial strain, pressure in our relationship, and the beginning development of questions about my ability to perform in my profession. I strained all of her great qualities to the limit.

Somehow the church was under the impression I was twenty-seven years old. I was only twenty-four. I don't think that was a welcomed revelation.

Our first Sunday there, only thirty-two people were on hand. There were a few young families, a few retired, or about to be retired couples, and some older single people. We did not see any changes right away.

It's an unusual thing about some small churches. They can be great places, or they can have the attitude of, "We were here long before you arrived. We will be here long after you leave, don't try to change anything, and don't upset anyone." They can be both of these at the same time. Church boards can be congenial, or unbelievably controlling, territorial, like they are the sole protector of some vast treasure, whose historical ways and memories must be protected at all costs. Most lie somewhere in between.

The town consisted of two major, intersecting highways. There was a town circle, almost like a round-a-bout. We lived on the only street in town. Our very nice parsonage was across the road from the church. Church members had built the house some years ago.

At the end of the road was a house and a butcher shop. While we were there, the school district built a brand new grade school between us and the butcher shop. It was great for the community. The young principal and I became friends. I don't remember who won our basketball games of horse, or one on one.

I went to the state house, not the religious organization, but the political one, as part of a citizen/professional educator's combo to talk about school funding. I got to speak to the high school football team once in awhile on Friday morning game days.

I reached out to the local Catholic community. They were a newer presence in the community. There were no joint services. I would have been run out of town.

We played in a couple's volleyball league. We did everything we could to be acclimated/assimilated to local life.

The town had a band. It played in the bandstand in the town circle. It was not of symphonic quality, but it was light years better than the Mayberry band of television infamy. We enjoyed being in the band, playing Souza marches for Friday night ice cream socials.

I was the director of a state wide church youth program. For one weekend, I even hired a pianist, and gave a religious music only, trumpet recital as a part of the services.

By fall, a few more people were in attendance, including some people with a no church background. That can be hard on a traditional congregation. We began to feel a little bit accepted and at home. There were always enough underlying situations that could make those moments fleeting.

Five months into this tenure, on Christmas weekend, on Sunday morning there were ninety-seven people in church. I think everyone was extremely happy about that. In that night's service, one of the men in the older age group stood up and said,"I thank God for our full church this morning, and for our young pastor." His thoughts, and few words carried more weight that anyone else in the church. The church bought us some nice luggage as a Christmas gift.

The increased attendance also brought a huge problem. There was no place to park. There was only one solution, short of losing people because they could not park. We had to tear up part of the parsonage lawn to put in parking.

Everyone was verbally polite, but the issue was very contentious. Feelings were very strong. There were only four votes against. A parsonage neighbor gave us an additional eighteen foot wide part of his lawn to provide more space. I knew better than to hold any kind of a ceremony or dedication for the opening of the parking lot, in deference to those who opposed it. My Christmas morning orator did not want the parking lot. He was always very kind.

On special occasion days, we would see one hundred twenty-five people in church. I think that was equal to about half the population of the town. Most of those who came in, filled in the missing age gap.

Peggy and I would have good days and bad days. There was still enough of a spark to keep things from completely unraveling. She grew up with a great respect for ministry. She hung in there, wishing life was different.

Sara was born. Labor was over thirty hours. Our doctor would not perform a C-section. Sara had a terrible, long case of colic. (is there any other kind?) Peggy had severe post-birth depression.

I had to ask for a raise. That was verboten. At one time I got a part time job (equally verboten). Rather than growing in popularity, or acceptance, the overall mood toward me began to go the other way. When they gave us the luggage the first Christmas it was a good joke that they definitely did not want us to use it. Before we left a little more than three years later, they did.

A good number of community people who were not from the church, came to our last service to say good-bye.

I was zero for three, not a very good batting average. Quitting was not an option. More than aspersions were cast at those who did.

CHAPTER ELEVEN | SWEET? HOME MINNESOTA

IT WAS NOT A GOOD SIGN. Our rental moving truck broke down after only sixty miles.We even had to change trucks. The in-laws were with us. Many times throughout the years, they came to help us move, sometimes this was hundreds and hundreds of miles. We always appreciated it.

We were on our way back to Minneapolis, (a suburb). I went to to work for a workaholic. This was someone Peggy and I knew well. I didn't ask for it, but he even put in writing that I would get a day off every week. Our bridesmaid friend was now the office manager in this church.

Peggy got a job running a business. Sara went to the church day care, (at that time, an answer to Sara's prayers.)

My job expanded a little bit over time, but the following is true: I was the church music director, the church youth director, the music education teacher for the Christian school, the choir director for the Christian school, the soccer coach for the Christian school, the state director for the teen contest program. I was on the board of a community organization that was similar to the Salvation Army. I was on the local television community access board. My schedule was seven days and six nights.

My salary was a nice step above my previous situation. We did not know until after we arrived, that the church had trouble meeting its budget.

Is it any wonder that Peggy and I reached our lowest point ever? Our premarital counseling advice about settling in for just a decent life together, was far better that our current situation. This was the love of my life. I never wanted anyone else. It was broken, and I had no idea what to do.

Before we got married I suggested the following: When times were good we would never joke about divorce. If times ever got tough, we would never talk about divorce. In later years, I have said " She stayed, we were too broke for her to leave."

The truth of the matter is. She was the person I knew she was when we got married, a person of great commitment, loyalty, and integrity. And obviously she still loved me, even though "the returns on her investment" were abysmal.

Seasonal music productions were expected. In our second year I did not do a major Easter production. I did not have the time, or the energy to do what it would take.

Peggy and I came to an agreement. If this (low key Easter performance) cost me my job, so be it. If I was unable to secure a permanent reduction to my schedule, I would resign. If things did not get better between us, I would resign. We would no longer sacrifice anything for our marriage.

So I boldly, (foolishly?) walked in to the office with the following scenario: "Either I get some time off, on a regular basis, or you will need to find me a good divorce lawyer, because I am going to need one." He sent us away on a week's vacation. It was a great week, but not a permanent fix.

Later that spring we took a vacation in Florida. It was our second time there. For years we had used vacation time to come back to Minnesota to see family. One year we went to Florida instead. It changed our life. We decided we would try not to be foolish, but would do some things along the way to enjoy life, to get away, to have some fun. This proved invaluable. Not every vacation turned out to be great, but most of them were.

We went to Florida. While there, we bought a one week time share, in Daytona. You could throw stones in the ocean from the balcony when the tide was in, (not that we ever did.) Rather than being burned, this was a great deal. It was very inexpensive. The fees stayed very low for almost twenty years. As an owner, sometimes other locations would give you a free week if you would sit through their presentation. You can also trade your week for a week in a different location. This gave us lots of vacation options. Sometimes we were able to give away one of our extra weeks.

We were able to use our Florida location some years. Most years, especially when the kids were younger, we traded it for some place within a one day's drive.

We arrived back home from the Florida vacation to find out I don't have a job. The board laid off two staff members due to financial pressures. I'm on unplanned sabbatical.

There was a church in Minneapolis called the Jesus People Church. During two summers (I think it was two), before college, my brother Steve and I used to go to the Park House. It was a midweek service in a house on Park Avenue, as a part of the then, new Jesus People Church.The worship surpassed any church worship I have ever witnessed, (then or now) on a regular basis. John Worre will always hold a special place in our hearts.

In college we were not really allowed to attend this church because it was not part of the organization. But now I could. We planned to visit many different places while I was unattached, but we just stayed at what was commonly called "JP," for short. The worship was still the same.

We worked. We struggled. Josiah was born. Everyone is a one of a kind. Some are more one of a kind than others. That fits Josiah, and I don't mean it in a bad way.

We have a staff pastor from the Jesus People Church, who we so highly respect and appreciate, come out to our house on a Sunday afternoon for his dedication. This is usually done as a part of a church service, but you know me, I buck tradition, and think I know a better way. (In the, it's a small world category, my sister Dawn, and this pastor got acquainted while working for the same missions organization, years later. This minister now attends Peggy's home church when he is not on an assignment.)

The dedication was great. We had some family and friends over. The pastor did not really know us on personal level. Yet during the dedication, he more or less tells us, "You're going to have to give this one up, (for the Gospel.) Are you willing?" We said yes.

There are many more books and chapters to be written in Josiah's life, but he has been all over the world, some of it as an international speaker, intercessor, for the Kingdom of God.

One of my goals for my kids is: I want more books to be written about them, than the ones they will write.

CHAPTER TWELVE | A MIRACLE

EVERYTHING IS STRETCHED and strained. Money is tight. No one is getting any sleep. Peggy has to start the process of going back to work after Josiah is born. Day care is a hassle, and super expensive. Some days when one of the kids are sick, we have a "debate" about whose job is more important that day, since one of us will have to stay home.

We have no idea what our future holds, absolutely no clue. We try to just put one day behind the current one, and one foot in front of the other.

I found a card. On the outside of the card was a heart, broken in two. The caption read, "I found this, does it belong to you?" Inside, the card simply said, "If it does, can I have it?" I don't remember exactly where that was in the healing process.

Somehow, we decided we were on the same team. We were broke, exhausted, and did not know how to get our life back on track, but over some time, the fighting eased.

Some of our fights were not much more than a long, sad silence. Our fights were kind. We did not yell or scream at each other. We didn't say things to be mean or spiteful. We did not try to wound each other with words. There were enough wounds already.

I don't think we ever argued in front of the kids. But kids are perceptive. Words may not be spoken. The kids may not be able to articulate, when they are young, but their spirit does get a general sense of the spirit of the house and its inhabitants.

I was not always a good person during some of these difficult times. I trusted her enough to tell her what was going on in my head. Just one of the issues was anger, and not a mild case.

I truthfully said that we never broke our vows about walking with God, and with each other. The truth also is, some of my walking with God was a little further back in the crowd. Everyone fights something in their own life. I am/was no different.

Some of this chapter could be in the second half of the book. I think the worship music at JP was a big help to us. It was unique in its Spirit. Even the kids responded to it, as it filled our home.

We also became impacted with the idea that God is a good God, and conversely, the devil is a bad devil. We were being challenged to believe in the goodness of God. This was a "different God" than the one I learned about in younger years.

The simple truth is, there was **Divine Intervention.** (We did keep ourselves in a place where God could reach us.) *God rescued us*, mended our fences, and our hearts, (with something much better, and more secure, than twine string.)

We both had to be willing to move forward, but I do really think God Himself rescued us. I really do think there was Divine intervention.

We once wondered if we were going to go through all of life in disillusionment. Graciously, genuine love returned, not the duty bound, "I'll stick with you whether I want to or not," kind of love.

Our relationship became better than we had ever known, and surpassed all of our expectations. There are several things that come across my mind every day. One of them is the grace and kindness I see every day in life of the love of my life.

CHAPTER THIRTEEN | THE END OF THE LINE

TIME LINE: IN BETWEEN CHURCHES (*We think*)

Place: Still in Minneapolis.

Ron was a good friend, and sometimes mentor before we moved back to Minnesota. He was a pastor in a neighboring town. When Peggy took the kids to see her parents one weekend, I told her I was going to call Ron. I did. It was good to hear from him, real good. He told me that the first church we went to after college, now needed a senior pastor. Ron still pastored his same church, these many years later.

I was excited. I called the "bishop." It was not the same one. The one I knew from our first trip to the state was retired. This was a bishop who knew not Brian, as in,

"A new king arose over Egypt, who did not know Joseph,"
Exodus 8:1.

This bishop told me our "first church" was well in to the selection process. He did not want to muddy the waters. I did not technically need his permission to contact the church, but thought it wise. I made an appeal. I told him I was there years ago. It might be the right situation for us and the church. Permission granted.

We flew in for an interview. We were invited back as the candidate for the church vote. This church was also under state directorship. The organization had final say, on everything, if necessary. Under normal circumstances, they let the church run their own affairs.

We had a Saturday night service. It went very well. A vote was taken after the Sunday evening service. It was unanimous. We were on the move again. And excited!

Peggy was seven months pregnant. I packed as much as I could and put it in storage. I flew out in early spring to begin pastoring. I came back to Minneapolis six weeks later to be there for the baby's birth. He was late.

He was a day and a half old before we named him. We took the naming of our children very seriously. We wanted to get it right. We named him Jonathan, Jonathan Robert. The Robert was after the name of our friend, who was now the senior pastor of the Jesus People Church.

I went back to pastor the church for a few weeks. When school was out, I returned to Minnesota to move the family. I flew Peggy and the baby out. My dad drove our car, with Josiah riding shotgun. I drove the moving truck. We flew my dad back to Minnesota.

Our first Sunday was also our twelfth anniversary. I gave Peggy flowers during the service and sang Billy Joel's *She's Got A Way About Her.*

I had been away for ten years. They had some growth and built a new building; but now, attendance had declined for a few years. My salary was good. The church budget was very tight. I needed to help the church rebound, and start a new chapter in church life.

Peggy would help me and be a stay at home mom. This was a major adjustment for all of us, and not a bad one. As fate would have it, several of my business friends wanted to hire her. This trip she was not looking for a job. With the house, the kids, and her ministry roles, she already had several. We were unable to sell our house in Minnesota. Neighborhood rules did not really allow us to rent it out. It's eventual sale took a huge burden off our shoulders.

Peggy had done the interviewing and hiring for the company she ran in Minneapolis. I remember she once told me that a person she interviewed and hired was not the same person who showed up for the job. That is, performance did not at all match the expectations anticipated due to the interview.

I think that is exactly how church leadership viewed me. I was not able to do enough to stabilize the attendance as needed. The leadership had worked so hard in previous years, they now wanted me do do the heavy lifting. New people came in. Not all of the old people stayed. Old leadership did not stay. I did some things well, some of the time.

We had lots of friends and lots of support. A lot of people were great, and extremely generous. Our kids had many unofficial grandparents. At one point, one lady even "ordered" me to send over my shirts, to be ironed and starched.

I just could not put the whole package of leadership, administration, services, ideas, creativity, advertising, and outreach together. I wanted to. I tried. It was not happening to the level of expectations.

Overall, marriage and family life was great. The kids were at an age, where almost every day had an aspect of "Magic" to it. At about the 13 year anniversary mark, I told Peggy we would do something special for our fifteenth anniversary. We wouldn't wait for our twenty-fifth. I told her i would buy her a new diamond ring, or take her anywhere in the 48 states for a vacation. In later years she told people she made the mistake of taking the trip. Of course I was never one hundred percent sure if that was said in jest.

As the fifteenth year drew closer, it was time to make plans. She asked if we could take the kids. She really is gracious and kind. The kids went with us. It was a great vacation.That location, and my choice of location to write this book, are the same. She eventually got the new diamond. She deserved it far in advance of its arrival.

One weekend, an unusually large number of people came to the Sunday night service, enough that Peggy took notice. Some were there who never came to church on Sunday night. Toward the end of the service I could literally smell the coffee, coming from another part of the building. I had pulled it off. After service I had scheduled a surprise birthday party for Peggy. Everyone in the church knew, except her.

Our family life was good. Overall, ministry was not as successful.

Our twins, Erik and Elijah were born. Having one baby is amazing. To have two at once was a special blessing beyond description. Some times I would just stare at them, if there was a remote chance they were sleeping. They were so different from each other. They still are.

We started home schooling, for a variety of reasons.

For a time we conducted our Sunday night service in English and Spanish. There was a very large migrant work force in the area.

We started a clothing ministry, in the church, for anyone who needed it. We were open Tuesdays. Everything was free.

Peggy led a young mom's Bible study. I played a little golf with some of the men in the church. My golfing was not much better than my baseball.

In the winter, I played basketball once a week with a bunch of men in the community. When Peggy found out we were playing full court ball, she had reservations. She wondered if I was too old.

Back up to our second arrival in town: Jonathan was the perfect baby and child. He never cried. He was happy. He was extremely generous. As a tiny child, he wanted to share his candy.

When I mowed lawn, he followed me around with his popcorn sounding mower. One evening while we ate, he asked if he could help me butcher the hedges next time. At first I had no idea what he meant. It dawned on me. The last time I cut the hedges, I had cut them really short. I must have told Peggy I butchered them.

We named all of our kids to not have nicknames. For instance, Josiah would never be called Joe. I intended to always call Jonathan exactly that, or even Jonathan Robert. One day at home someone called him Johnny. I wasn't fond of that, but agreed they could call him Jon. It fit. He was known as Jon from that day on.

We were teaching him the twenty-third Psalm. He said it this way: "The Lord is my Shepsherd. I not shall want." That is the only way he would say it.

When the twins were born, it appeared that Jon thought he was kicked out of the nest too soon.

A lot of family life was magical. I was so proud of Sara and the boys. When Sara was born Peggy wanted a girl. She really wanted a girl. (After all the kids were on hand, she found out that she was/is a boys mom.) We never wanted to know, boy or girl, prior to birth. Two days before she was born I bought her a little kid's book about Abraham.

RE Sara: Peggy had some stomach X-rays to find out why she was not feeling well. We did not yet know she was pregnant. Once we did, the doctor immediately wanted us to abort her. He said he could almost guarantee she would be missing limbs, parts of limbs, or have other severe developmental issues. She was perfect.

Here is just one item to indicate that Sara is not missing anything. When she was sixteen, her lady boss took her to Chicago to help select wedding dresses for the bridal salon where Sara worked.

Water Colored Ponies: Wayne Watson

As the family grew I was reminded every day, of this song, which I loved. Part of it said: "There are water colored ponies on my refrigerator door….. They look a little less like little boys every day."

Family life was kind of the opposite of my professional life. The church mortgage was always a struggle. It was a perfect dichotomy. One part of life was great, enjoyable. The other was a struggle. Why couldn't I get all of my ducks in a row?

I did two things to anger the bishop. That's never good. On one of them, I was in consultation with him, and thought I had, if not his blessing, at least his permission. I thought wrong. Issue number two: For the other one, my heart and my motives were pure, but I had go to the capitol (of the organization) before him and a state leadership committee and make an apology.

They found out I did not properly appreciate (it was true) the organization's national publication. I had shared an instance in particular with the congregation. It was just a theological interpretation issue. Another pastor, not that far away from me, had written a rather scathing editorial note, which was published. He did not have to apologize.

I worked closely with the president of the local financial institution that held the church mortgage. In a worst case scenario, the state organization was on the books for the mortgage. The lending institution worked out a verbal agreement with me on a refinancing that we could handle. I was to present this to the bishop after an annual meeting that was held for all churches, staff, and board members in the area. I never got the chance.

The first thing he said was, "You're done. I'm going to make a leadership change in your church." Some terms for my departure were quickly spelled out. I was furious. In the back of my mind I knew this was a possibility. The reality was harsh. We were allowed some transition time. A few months before this, the bishop had been at an area meeting of all of our local churches. He verbally prayed for every church and pastor, except me. Was it an innocent oversight? Was it a purposeful, hidden message?

If a vote would have been taken by the church, it still would have been unanimous, for us to stay. It was just different people, and not enough of them. For a fleeting moment the idea of taking the church private crossed my mind. The question was asked. I knew it was not the right thing to do. I said, I could not do that. I have never regretted the decision.

During my adult life, my dad did not initiate communication with me. Neither did the bishop. I had offered to meet with an organizational official for mentoring. It never happened.

Was the bishop right? There was a lot of debate about that. I did not see it that way for a long time. A real long time. I had respect for his office. I did not have respect for him. It's not fair to say, and not accurate, but I saw my first bishop as a prophet. I saw the second one as an MBA. That was my problem, not his. I was angry at him, very angry. I was angry at the few people that appeared to want to make life difficult for me. (I was plenty capable of doing that on my own.)

Most Christians are great people. They are not out to "get" anyone. I think it is like most situations/organizations/businesses/families/etc, where it can be the the few: those who make the most noise can sometimes do the most damage.

God took care of us. It was not quite like Israel leaving Egypt with the spoils of Egypt, (Exodus 3:21-22.) but we were blessed. I had a pastor acquaintance/friend in a town about an hour away. We went to his church one Sunday, before we moved away. We did not speak before the service. He did not know why we were there there. He took an offering for us.

Before we moved, I took a week, rented a car, and went to Minneapolis to look for a job. I needed to find something as a safety net in case no other doors opened. I knew I couldn't stay in the state we were in. Neither did we want to.

I went knocking. The minister who dedicated the twins, had come to preach for us for several days. He was a distant state director himself. He headlined our church's 50th Anniversary Celebration.

A famous leader had been at the Jesus People Church more than once as a guest speaker. (He of the God is a good God…the devil is a bad devil messages.) He was once scheduled to come to our church for several days, but his dad passed away during this scheduled time. He never made it.

Many months before this, during one prayer time the verse about casting mountains in to the sea, came to mind. I did not know if the building (The source of the large mortgage) would be in a nearby lake when I woke up the next morning or not. Instead of the building being gone, I was gone.

I contacted both of these men about any openings in their state. I had a connection in the greater Chicago area. I spent some time with him. I went to the State office in Minnesota and Wisconsin. No doors opened.

During one long walk, Peggy begged me, "Can't we just go someplace we have never been, and start over"? She was always the adventurous one. With five kids, and the unknown, that idea of going to "pan for gold" scared me to death. I knew I could at least get a job in Minneapolis, if necessary. (My week's trip there was successful.) It's back to Minnesota.

In the past, I was given access to three national leaders. They invested in me. I was given a front row seat, behind the scenes access, back stage passes. I could not translate what I had seen and heard in to what I needed to do.

In boxing, amateur bouts are limited to three rounds. I know at least some professional fights go twelve or fifteen rounds.

A fight can end one of many ways. The referee can stop the fight at any time, look in a boxer's eyes to see if anybody's home, and stop the fight if he does not like what he sees. (I think the bishop's summation was, "There's nobody home.") The referee can stop the fight if he thinks one fighter is taking too much of a pounding, even if the fighter is still on his feet.

Some fights have a mandatory, standing eight count, if one of the boxers is knocked down, even if he bounces right back to his feet. If a fighter is knocked down, and is groggy, he has ten seconds to regain his composure and his senses, and the fight can be resumed.

To my way of thinking, if he had any sense why would he be there in the first place? I mean, where is the sense in volunteering to get your head beaten to a pulp? Even an inferior opponent is going to land some of his punches on your jaw.

A fight ended by the referee in these circumstances is called a technical knockout. If a fighter is knocked down, loses consciousness, and does not get up, it is called a knockout, and there is nothing technical about it. A boxer is known by his won/loss record. His prowess is measured by how many technical knock outs (TKO's) and knockouts he has inflicted on his opponents. They are always listed with the won/loss record.

There's only one more problem, a very important one, By this time, I was mad at God. It's not like that hasn't happened to anyone before. See David in 2 Samuel 6:8.

Had I misread the call altogether? Had I just failed? What was I supposed to do now?" Where was I supposed to go in life? It would take years for me to sort this out, to find some answers.

So here I am, face down on the canvas, down for the count. I am not getting up. If you are totally unfamiliar with boxing, the canvas is the surface you walk on (bouncing on your toes of course) during the fight. Your goal is to keep the canvas about six feet away from your eyes. (I don't see anything "artistic" about this canvas.)

When Job's life fell apart he "fell to the ground and worshipped," (Job 1:20,) He said, "blessed be the name of the Lord," 1:21, and "did not sin nor did he blame God," Job1:22. My response was not that good. Job's wife said to him, "Curse god and die." Job 2:9. My response was not that bad. I know, it never does any good to compare ourselves to other people. See Jesus' analysis of the Pharisaical prayer in the New Testament.

CHAPTER FOURTEEN | INTERLUDE

WHEN I GOOGLE INTERLUDE, the first synonym given is interval, then intermission. It is given in reference to a theatrical or orchestral performance. Years ago, when Peggy and I were at a minister's retreat, we heard a very well known pastor talk about a difficult time in his life. He told his wife, "I can't wait until this is over, so we can get this show back on the road." His wife wisely said to him, "I think this is the show."

At the beginning of this part of life we did not know if we were in an interlude, or if "This was the show." Turns out, "It was the show."

My brother Scott was the music director at a church in the southern Minneapolis metro. This kind senior pastor took me under his wing, and called me his education minister. I played trumpet as a part of Scott's worship team. This was very part time. It was my last staff position. Life evolved, it moved on. Ministry as I knew it was done. It was not a conscious decision. It just kind of happened.

I was inactive. I sent a note with the resignation of my credentials to the state director (of Minnesota). He's a great man. He just retired. His replacement is a childhood friend of mine, from where else?–camp. I never made an intentional decision to step away. It just seemed to be the way life went. There were some doors open, but none that could provide the support I needed to take care of my family.

I had a "lost year" time wise, where all I did was work. As time went on that eased some what. Even though we did not understand everything, there seemed to be more blessing in our new, fledgling life, than in our old one. It didn't make me any happier or any less angry. I still had not figured anything out, about life or our situation

We went to a "Faith Church" for a year. (More on that subject later.) It was too far away. We went to a great, well established, highly esteemed church from our organization. Nothing was wrong with it. It just was not for us. We ended up at a local church we really liked. The senior pastor was a skilled trumpeter. I arranged some duets for us.

We bought a house. My in-laws helped all of their kids with housing. They helped us with the down payment. My father-in-law is a skilled carpenter. He always built houses in addition to his full time job. He built many, many houses for he and his wife, the last one at age 72.

I came off the road from a sales job. I needed a job. I answered an ad in the paper, (back when they still did that sort of thing.) I got hired at a manufacturing plant on the west side of the metro, third shift. On my first night, a guy with long, blond, curly hair, and a full bushy beard lets me in to the building. He looks like he just came from a Grateful Dead concert. I think to myself, "Hey, you know, this could be all right."

My dad spent twenty-five years making "Cream of Wheat" for Nabisco. He retired young, to go back to the farm. My father-in-law retired, young, from General Motors. He would do construction part time, if he wanted to. I had been through two manufacturing plants as a tourist. Going in, I had no concept of what was included in this industry.

Marathon Man

My pay rate for my new job was not that great, but they were so far behind on orders, the whole company was on a mandatory 48 hours. They were paying double time for anything over 48 hours with a maximum of twelve hours a day allowed. I worked fifty-seven days straight, (not all of them were twelve hour shifts,) took only three days off during my first one hundred days, and then we took a vacation. I was partly proud of that record, and partly needed to repent.

I've always told my boys, what's most important regarding money is not what you make per hour, but what you make per year.

I had been in some kind of supervision/management my whole life. My first four months of hard work paid off. When a supervisor's job opened up, I applied, and was accepted. The raise was great, and the boss gave another increase at years' end.

The kids went back to public school. Peggy went back to work outside of the home. She did not want to go back to the office or the corporate world. She went into retail management and had a great career.

We went to church. The kids grew. My thoughts about God never stopped. I worked nights. I went home, took the kids to school, got a nap, got up to pick the kids up from school, sometimes got another nap and went to work. Life was definitely not all bad. Peggy and I were good.

I originally went to work nights to keep the twins out of day care. I had always been a night person. As a teenager I listened to radio stations from Minneapolis,

Chicago, and others across the country, deep in to the night. That is, once I put the trumpet, guitar, and piano to rest for the night. Some people have pets. I had instruments, which were equally loved. They did not have to be walked in the middle winter nights when it was thirty degrees below zero.

As a kid, if I had homework, it usually got placed on top of the piano on my way in the door. It usually only got picked up on my way out the door in the morning, and finished during first hour history.

If sleep deprivation and coffee would kill you, I would have been dead decades ago. I have always been able to go without sleep. It's not a talent. I was born that way. So was my dad.

I enjoyed the nights at work. You missed some of the politics and chaos of the days. Production quotas were the same for all shits. Slacking off was not allowed. Some of the work included parts coming out of a machine at a set pace whether you were ready or not. Most night workers were not as uptight. Some were definitely characters. Once in a while during the summer months I would arrive home to find the boys still up. I asked the, "Why? question. The reply was, "Because we can."

We were a high tech plastics injection molding company. Some parts were measured fifty different ways, within two thousandths of an inch. We were an original equipment supplier to the microelectronics industry. We had lots of patents. Our products had to work. If they did not, millions of dollars could be on the line for our customers. Imagine our delight, when we saw one of our products on TV as a part of an ad. We were not mentioned by name, but we knew they were ours. Even just recently, I saw one of this company's products in a production shot of a mega conglomerate in a financial magazine.

I did love my company. For years it was a great place to work. It was a private company. The two men who ran it were great men and great business men. It was very much an employee based company. Every quarter everyone was eligible for a two week bonus. We got that bonus, four or five quarters in a row, more that once.

I worked on my theology. The previous years were extremely harsh on it. Peggy and I talked together about it many times. Questions were there: Where was God? Why did He not do something? Why did He not do more? Does He care?

I was very familiar with Psalm 73. In fact I was very familiar with the whole Bible. I knew the words. I had a long way to go to learn what they meant and how they needed to be applied to my life and my future. I was never perfect, but there were times, when I knew my heart and motives were pure, that it appeared God did not intervene, (as I thought He should.)

Psalm 73:13 says, "Surely in vain have I kept my heart pure, and washed my hands in innocence." Verse 16b says, It was troublesome in my sight." I was aware of the punishment, the destruction in the end for the wicked, v. 18. I could not wait until the end. If anyone in my life needed to receive retribution, how was that going to help me?

I came to the conclusion that I should have obtained a music degree, and stayed in Minnesota after college. I always ended up there anyway. I should have written music and upped my game to become a better performer.

All of my brothers and sisters are Christians. I/we discussed some of this with them. My brother Steve was kind. He very much disagreed with the previous paragraph.

I came to the conclusion that God just did not intervene that much in daily life. I was treading on thin ice. Minnesotans know a lot about that. Every year cars and boats and ice houses (for winter fishing) go through the ice, in to the lake. Incorrect thinking about God can lead to far more serious consequences than losing a car in the drink, (slang phrase for anything lost to the water.)

I especially could not reconcile the lack of results when my heart was pure. At least some of the time, I could not point to any major deficiencies in my thoughts or character that would limit positive results.

That wasn't always the case. During some of the interlude years that was a struggle. No one is ever perfect, but at least some of the time I was doing well. If I had the whole cause and effect thing figured out to perfection, I would sell millions of books and be on every TV show in the country.

So what did I do? I started over. I knew I was still a Christian. I once told someone at work, I may be the worst Christian you will ever meet, but I'm still a Christian. I started over with everything but that one truth. I was not totally foolish. I knew that the life, death for my sin, and resurrection of Jesus were unarguable facts of life and theology. Everything else was fair game.

I knew there were times when God intervened in my life in the past. I knew His presence was real. I knew my call was real, even if I did not understand it. Imagine how much it meant to me, years later when a new friend,

Brent, who knew nothing of my story said "God's not sorry He called you in to ministry."

I knew God was real. I also knew the devil was real. My foot was healed when I was fourteen. I had an experience with the devil when I was about seven. I woke up one night, thinking I was dead, and he (the devil) was there. I saw a clear vision of Jesus one night when I was eight. I heard angels singing when I was about fourteen. The song was, "Great Is Thy Faithfulness." (All good music comes from heaven.)

I had a plan. I read my Bible as if I were reading it for the first time. I prayed as if I knew nothing about prayer. Maybe I didn't. I put all of my past theology aside. I put all of my sermons aside. I put most of my past experiences aside. I put Biblical interpretive ideas aside, preconceived and otherwise. I started over with everything except salvation faith.

The crazy work hours did not last real long. That industry is very cyclical. When work calmed down to forty hours a week I got a part time job as well. A house and cars and five kids was a handful.

The company I worked for was not the same. It was still good, but they felt the need to go public. That hurt some. They did a merger with a company they had started years ago. That hurt some more. The two men who had run the company for a couple of decades retired. Years later, after another merger/buyout, most of the jobs went overseas and the corporate headquarters (under new management) took the last train for the coast, (East coast, Boston area.) (Side note: Jon is fourteen. He has a seventeen year old friend who drives his parents new SUV. We never meet him.)

CHAPTER FIFTEEN | FAMILY REUNION

FOR A TIME I HAD A FIFTH SON, JOSH. For a time I had a fifth son, Josh. He was between the twins and Jon in age. He was always at the house and always welcome.

Our twenty-fifth wedding anniversary party, held at our house, was one of the great days of our life. Josh's mom helped host. So did Sara's best friend Rachel. Relatives came from Verndale. A lot of Peggy's relatives came from out of state. Friends came from work. Dannie (from camp,) and wife Marcie were there. It was so much fun.

A year later we took a weekend trip to Peggy's home town. It was a good trip. A couple of weeks later we are sitting in a Chi Chi's restaurant, (I miss that one.) It was just the two of us. I asked if she wants to move back to her home town. Her parents and her brothers all lived there. She had not lived closer than three hundred miles to her parents in her entire adult life. Her first response was, "maybe."

I had a favorite carpet installer from my floor coverings sales days. He put in new carpet. Peggy's dad installed new sliding glass doors to the deck. The house went on the market. It sold very quickly and a closing date was set. The move is a belated, 25th Anniversary present/ thank you to Peggy.

I had gone on ahead to get a job. Peggy was able to do a transfer with her company. We moved the day after Thanksgiving. I put Jon in charge of stacking everything in the truck. He was superb.

We bought a house from her parents that they had just built. The job I landed did not last. I was promised forty hours. I got it for the first two weeks. The manager then says no deal to the guaranteed forty hours. This is not looking good. I got a different job. I found an additional weekend job. I eventually ended up with a commission sales job in the floor covering industry. My sales were not strong enough.

We are bleeding cash and going through profits from the sale of our house. Through the years I had given the kids a multi-book list to read to help give them a good financial education. One of them was the Cash Flow Quadrant, by Robert Kiyosaki. It talks about four different ways people earn money, and of course, the importance of positive cash flow. Its message was all too clear to me.

I got to spend a little time helping my father-in-law with the next to last house he built. Peggy loved her job in her new location. Sara had been on her own for quite some time. She did not make the move with us. Josiah was out of high school and in and out of the house at times.

Peggy had a great time. She was able to spend more time with her parents and extended family. I finally learned my way around her home town.

I can get in the car and drive across the country, with a map, but if I come to your house, go inside, and am there for an hour, I will have no idea what direction I came from, when I get in my car. My friend Pastor Sam, coined the phrase "spacial dyslexia" to describe my condition. I am legendary for it, in hospitals, malls, and leaving new restaurants.

We eventually settled in to a community church that I think had ties to the Willow Creek "Super Church" in Illinois. I played keyboard for their very early, traditional service, and my trumpet during their contemporary service.

God Rest Ye Merry Instrument...

I broke some dental work while playing in church one Sunday, and slowly, the trumpet playing faded out. In later years, I really did not have a good place to practice. It makes a lot of noise.

At different times, two of the boys decided they were going to take trumpet lessons from dad. I never pushed them. Sara took some piano lessons, but our kids just never showed that much interest in playing an instrument. The boys assumed they could almost immediately play like dad. Neither one came back for the second lesson. None of my dad's boys became boxers. None of my boys became musicians. Their undeveloped musical genius is resting comfortably, somewhere out of sight and out of earshot.

As I write this, the trumpet family heirloom is now at Elijah's place. He has a *'Trumpet For Beginner's'* book by Dr. Bruce Pearson, (imagine that!).

Old Folks At Home...

We talked to my brother Steve about he and his wife coming to see us on a weekend. A date is arranged. When they arrive, they are the last to arrive. What Steve does not know, is that his dad, and all of his brothers and sisters are there for his 50th birthday party. We had a wonderful, fun weekend. Not all of it was at his expense. I bought him a nice card. I also bought him a second card to razz him about his old age.

Peggy does not like surprises. For her fiftieth birthday I planned something special. I did not tell her. She caught me cleaning house. That right there would give her a stroke if she were not healthy. She said, "What's going on?" I told her, your best friend and entire family are about two hours away. They'll be here for your birthday. That surprise was acceptable.

I kept in touch with my old job from Minneapolis, and talked to them occasionally.

CHPATER SIXTEEN | PRELUDE

TIME FRAME, IN MINNEAPOLIS, before the move to Peggy's home town. Erik can throw a baseball, with great distance and velocity. We had a little plastic golf cart toy. Erik is standing in the street. The golf cart is up by the house. He is just little, but he is knocking down that golf cart by throwing a baseball at it. Even though he was not a big kid, he used to get ribbons in city wide, summer, grade school track meets for his baseball throwing ability.

Jon played one year of Little League baseball. He had great, although raw, talent. He had a pure, sweet swing that people would kill for. He only played one year. Through the years I told the boys that Erik should be pitching in the majors, to Jon. I even told them the minimum major league salary, but alas, it was not pursued.

During Jon's year of Little League, he wanted me to buy him an eighty dollar bat. At the time the three hundred dollar saxophone illustration rolled through my mind. I said no to the bat. Jon was furious. He was just turning ten. When I left for work that night I said, "I'll see you in the morning." His response was, "No you won't cause I won't be here." Where was the little boy with the lawn mower?

Before moving to Peggy's home town, Jon went to a weekly youth group with one of his school friends, whose dad was the pastor of a small church.

Jon ran an unofficial bike shop out of our garage. There were enough bike parts to furnish the whole Tour de France for replacement supplies. Jon was an extremely gifted bike rider and skate boarder. I heard a lot about

Tony Hawk in those days. When we moved, there were more tires, rims, and frames in our garage than you could believe.

Jon always, always wore a hat. Later on, one night at dinner at grandpa's it became quite an issue. Jon kept the Fox company in business.

Jon used to ridicule what he termed the losers, the teens who hung around on the corners of the street, who smoked, cigarettes and otherwise.

Jon worked at Burger King before we moved. That got him a job at Wendy's in our new location, Peggy's hometown. Jobs for teens were almost impossible, but he had one. He had a great sense of humor. He could have done stand up. His perfect impressions of the customers kept us in daily stitches.

When the boys were much younger, Josiah could free hand draw all of the characters from the Jungle Book movie, with precision. Jon could act them all out, with equal precision. Eventually he became too self conscious to perform.

I did not have many rules for the kids while they were at home but I was not very flexible about the ones I had. They were, no smoking, no alcohol, no drugs. Keep the police and social services out of my life. Go to church with us. My last rule was, you just have to be a decent human being, as in, a little kindness, a little gratitude, and maybe even a little deference once in awhile.

There was a show on TV a few years ago called The Mentalist. On one episode the subject of high school came up. The main character said, "I never went to high school." When questioned, he said " I was busy." That was Jon.

I would take him to school. (now in Peggy's home town.) They had a open lunch. Students could leave the school during the lunch hour, and he did. The plan was, the students come back to school after lunch. Jon failed that part of the agreement. He didn't come back. Some days he did not make it as far as lunch.

The school would call. We would go to the office, affirm our belief in, and commitment to, education. To make matters worse, the state had a tough truancy law. Parents could be hauled in to court and fined for their kids' unexcused absenteeism. We were worried. Would **that** phone ring or would a summons appear in the mail?

I was reading a magazine in the mid 1980's. I came across an article. It was about a man who was then one of, if not **the** country's leading rocket scientists. He was the son of one of grandpa Howard's brothers. He was my mom's first cousin. True story. I remember hearing about his academic advances during my youth. The science gene completely missed me. I really mean, completely.

Jon never had a science course, at any level that he couldn't teach. In fact, I don't think he had any course that he couldn't teach. By the time he was to enter what was supposed to be his senior year, he took some aptitude tests. He had, I suppose, a ninth grade education. He tested out at third year college for math. His other scores were mostly the same. He really was a true genius.

He found out he could go to the local community college for two hours a day, five days a week, and graduate with his class. He said, "I can do that." He went for two weeks, and no more.

His actions at home betrayed his intellectual capacity. Before long, he broke all of my rules. One time he would not go to church with us. When he refused, I escorted him out of the house, and locked it, as the rest of us went to church. When we returned home, he was not there. Neither were a couple of his brother's possessions. Jon had returned home earlier, and removed the possessions, Both Jon and the possessions did return home.

Eventually Jon completely broke his relationship with us. I don't think he ever planned, or said, "I'm going to destroy mom and dad's household and life," but it appeared to be his mission. Drugs had taken hold of him.

In response to some of his dealings, (in the literal sense, definitely no pun intended,) our house and yard were vandalized. Windows were broken. People we did not know came to the door, demanding money, or to see him.

I challenged Jon every step of the way. I literally told him he picked the wrong dad. I was not going to let him go easily or quietly. He had a probation officer. He was in juvenile detention. I told him they should name a wing of the detention center in his name. He was there often enough. He missed his mom's special birthday, and the friends that came to visit us. They were his friends too. He was in detention.

He was always all angry and vociferous during his first couple days of detention. As the drugs wore off he became more mild, calmer, conversational, bordering on rational.

Jon drank coffee. Before, during, and after he tore his life apart, he and I would go to the local Oasis. (Yes, just like the Garth Brooks song, there really was an Oasis restaurant, out by the interstate.) They were open twenty-four hours and I could get marmalade on my toast.

He and I would sit for hours and discuss life's issues. He communicated on an adult level, most of the time.

We continued this practice while his life was in shambles. Our entire life was precarious. Would Jon do something that could not be undone? What further damage would he do to his, or his brothers' lives? We feared for his life, and on one occasion, for our own lives.

If you asked Jon a question, he would tell you the answer. If he did not know the answer, he would tell you the answer anyway. He would make it up as he went along. Before he was done, he had you and himself convinced that he was right. Every once in awhile, I would stop him mid soliloquy, and say, "No, Jon." When he knew he'd been had, he would just quietly grin.

Jon had a serious girlfriend. They were already planning to spend the rest of their lives together. We loved her.

Even in difficult times, the coffee, and sometimes very late bites to eat, continued. I really did invest every ounce of time and energy I had. Without the drugs we got along great. I enjoyed my time with him.

He struggled with God, religion, faith. He trusted me enough to tell me about this. I was a safe place for his questions, discussions and views. I never yelled, belittled him, or made him feel any less valued.

At home, there were heated arguments between us, but thirty minutes later we would be sitting downstairs in his room. He would quietly listen to everything I had say.

Because of his volatility, and the extreme stress he brought to our house, I made a demand. I told him he could only say what he really meant. There was to be no reading between the lines. He was not allowed to say something outrageous, and then later say he was just kidding.

One night he threatened the family with the ultimate violence. I actually asked Peggy to take the twins and get out of the house and call the police. When the police arrived, as much as I could, I demanded that they take him away. I told them I did not want him in my house any more, ever. They would not do it. It was a tough night.

More than once I had to leave work to address a serious situation. I wanted to emancipate Jon. In that state it was almost impossible. We didn't. We/he couldn't meet all of the criteria. We even stopped at an out of state military prep school once, to look it over.

As the apostle John finishes writing his Gospel, he makes a summary. He suggests, that if all the works of Jesus were written in detail, the world itself would not contain the books which were written, (John 21:25.) The whole world wouldn't be able to contain the volume. There is a lot more I could say about Jon and the tumult he created, but I think you have a clear enough picture.

Midnight Train To Georgia...by James P Weatherly

One night, on the way to my weekend job, (a forty mile, one way trip,) I called my old boss at my old job in the Twin Cities. She said," Brian, God must love me. The guy who replaced you when you left, just turned in his notice. Do you want your old job back?" I don't think she expected me to say yes. I said, "I don't know, maybe." I knew.

I was hoping that temporarily, this would be Peggy's favorite song. There's a line in the song that says, I'd rather live with him in his world, than live without him in mine. I never needed to ask, but I was thinking, "I'm going back to Minneapolis. (there were multiple reasons.) I really, really want you to come with me, but I'm going back to Minneapolis. As an aside, her parents had already moved, 150 miles away.

I started in late October. I slept on the floor behind Sara's couch in her condo. I got my exact same job back, same rating. I looked for housing. I went home most weekends. Sound familiar? (One time the office I reported to was a block and a half from my dad's old Creme of Wheat plant. It really is a small, circular world.)

We unloaded our truck in a Minneapolis suburb (one we had not lived in before, if you can believe that,) the night before Christmas Eve. It was zero degrees with a howling wind. It was about midnight before the truck was unloaded. The in-laws and two of my brothers helped unload. It might have been our worst move ever. I was on a no sleep binge.

Sara did all of the cooking, and hosting for the Christmas Eve meal, our main holiday event. We met her future fiancé. She saved our life.

Jon did not make the trip. He was still a minor. It was a potential powder keg on a variety of levels.

CHAPTER SEVENTEEN | THE PHONE CALL

I WENT TO GET JON AND BROUGHT him back to Minneapolis. There was a possibility he would stay. He didn't. Erik and I took a trip to see him. I bought him a bunch of clothes, shoes, etc.

In February Peggy and I went to see him. He needed some legal help. For the first time, he was different. He was apologetic. He said "Dad, you are right, about everything. I'm going to change my life." I really think he tried.

Sara went to see him in May for his eighteenth birthday. He was glad to see her. They were very close. He was not doing that well.

Wish I didn't know now what I didn't know then…
Bob Seeger.

I was in my car, sitting outside a hospital in downtown Minneapolis. Josiah went in to the hospital pharmacy to get a prescription he needed. My phone rang. The voice on the other end of the line said, "Jon Died".

There are no words. I tell Josiah. I won't pretend to say I know what went through his mind. It's my birthday.

Jon's girlfriend had gone home about 12:30 AM. I think it was about noon the next day, she went see him. She found him. He was still holding an iced tea in his hand. It was an overdose.

I was the minister at many funerals. Some were strangers. Some were dear friends. Some were like grandparents to my children. I was with a mom when she made the decision to discontinue life support for her six year old son. I have helped families pick out caskets and burial plots. I have tried to conduct a service where families, weeping, override my voice.

With all of that said, there is no way to prepare for this. Everything wants to be a blur. Yet the circumstances demand critical thinking, a clear head, rationalization, resolve, and very fast decision making.

Legally, an autopsy had to be performed. His body had to be transported across state lines. Finding a home church had been a long process. We thought we had made a decision, but weren't sure. The church's new pastor had only been there two weeks. We basically are without a church or a minister. The irony is not lost on me.

My brother Scott had a connection to a funeral home. It was the right one. The funeral home director, recommended a minister from his church. He was the perfect one.

Sara, Josiah, and I drove back to where we used to live to hold a wake for Jon. All of the phones are going nonstop during the trip.

The church we had attended is able to host a wake for us. With less than a twenty-four hour notice, 50 kids show up. One doesn't. He has already admitted himself to rehab. As I hear the names of some of these people, there are some which I do not know. I also realize that a lot of the dealers from the greater area are there. I had heard their first names from Jon.

The authorities must have known this. Everyone was left alone. Some of Jon's friends got memorial tattoos. Some of them made the trip to Minneapolis for the funeral.

From a prior reference: The seventeen year old friend who drove his parent's SUV? Jon later told me it was not his parent's vehicle. It was his. We don't know for sure when the drug use started, but he was at least exposed to it too long before anyone knew.

At the time of Jon's death, I already had a new boss at work. He was by now also a friend. He was great. I knew the Chairman of the Board and the CEO of my company a little bit on a personal basis. Lots of people did. I once had a long chat with the CEO on what had been kind of a tough day for both of us. He said I made his day.

The company matched any funds collected from co-workers. The CEO sent the check, and a very nice note to me.

Peggy and Sara wrote the greatest eulogy I have ever heard. The pianist, from the "borrowed" church, picked just the right music. The minister was absolutely heaven sent. The funeral was filled with memories of all the good that was once in Jon's life, and all of the joy he brought to our family in earlier days.

The funeral was held at the funeral home chapel. A lot of people from work came. It touched my heart. So many people attended, that we did not have enough time to talk to them all, as we wanted. There was not enough time for me to say goodbye to Jon, with or without anyone there. This brings other tears.

A reception was held in a church a few blocks away. Sara's friend Rachel (from the anniversary party) took care of all of the arrangements for the food. She saved our life. Years later, we ended up living across the street from that church.

Jon loved children. He is buried as close as possible to the "Little Angels" section of the cemetery, in front of a tree. We refer to it as "Jon's tree."

It was a cool, crisp fall day at the cemetery. Jon literally took his hat to his grave. He was buried in one of his hats. The weather did not bother me. By the end of the service, it was not the weather that made me numb. They were about to put my son in the ground. "Out of the depths have I cried to thee, Lord hear my voice." Psalm 130:1. During one of my later solo trips to Kansas City (in a future chapter) I simply asked God to cry with me.

I now had a new meaning to the valley of the shadow of death. This was not the shadow. This was the real thing. It stung. Hard. I did not blame God. I was not angry at God for this.

Everyone was so kind and thoughtful during this time. I think we knew the following truth before, but we came to the realization that, "Everyone as a story." Everyone has something in life that is extremely difficult. They shared their stories, not to complain, but to let us know they had an understanding, and would unite with us, in our grief.

No one said anything stupid, or hurtful. Through the years, one of the less informed things I heard at funerals, way too many times, was, "I guess God needed him (or her) a lot more than we did." I do not know all of the reasons people die, but I do know, that is not one of them.

Our friend from our first pastorate, the one who appreciated the full house on Christmas morning, had lost an adult son to a car crash. I remember how broken he was, in telling the story, even twenty years later.\

I remember exactly when, after these events when I said to Peggy, "I'm done with parenting. If I could, I would just walk away. (not from Peggy, but from parenting) I've had it. I can't do this any more." A long time ago Sugar Ray Leonard fought Roberto Duran in a highly anticipated (hyped) boxing match. I expected Duran to win, but after one of the rounds he said "no mas." (no more.) I was ready to say "no mas" to parenting. I didn't. You can't.

Peggy and I committed to each other that we would stand together in this uncharted territory. We did. I told the twins I would do my absolute best to be the dad they still needed. They still deserved a father.

A parenting story comes to mind. I had a friend named Bryan (he was J. Brian. I was Brian J.) who came to the funeral. Bryan was an old work friend from a former life, as in, a long time ago.) I performed a wedding ceremony once for him. I had become friends of his family.
Bryan had two little kids. He asked his dad, "When does parenting get easier?" Bryan knew the answer, before his dad said a word, when he saw his dad's wise, all knowing smile. Of course the answer was, "It doesn't."

Now is the time for a Bible story. Joseph, the eleventh of twelve sons had dreams. He would one day rule over all of them. His brothers were not particularly enthralled with his dreams. They sold him to slavery, to some Egyptians. His master's wife falsely accuses him of an attempted physical assault. He is wrongly thrown in prison. Because he can interpret dreams for Pharaoh, he becomes the leader of the entire kingdom, under only Pharaoh.

I believe it was thirteen years from the time he was sold to slavery until he becomes the ruler of the land. In Genesis 41:51 he says, "God has made me forget all my trouble and all my father's household."

This is what happened to me with the marriage difficulty of many years gone by. I forgot it, as if it never happened. The pain was gone. This really helped the two of us in our approach to life, following Jon's death. We were in uncharted territory.

There is a more troubling Bible story for me, from the same time. Joseph's brothers have to go to Egypt to buy food. There is a great, seven year famine. Israel does not have food. Egypt does, because of Joseph's wisdom and leadership.

The brothers stand before Joseph. They do not recognize him. He knows them. He asks about their family. He tells them that the next time they come for food, they have to bring their youngest brother with them.

Jacob, the dad, has already lost Joseph. The brothers told Jacob, that he was killed by an animal. After much pleading, Jacob lets Benjamin, the youngest brother, go. Judah, one of the sons, guarantees Benjamin's safe return.

During the return meeting Joseph has a plan to retain only Benjamin. Judah, fearing the reaction of his father Jacob, says to Joseph, "How shall I go up to my father if the lad is not with me?"

I had a dream, some time after Jon's death. I saw only his face. He looked good, happy. The most important question in all of my life is, "How shall I go up before my Father, and the lad be not with me?" The truth of the matter is, I don't know where Jon is. His lifestyle and attitude did not give any indication of a good ending.

Did his turnaround in February last? Did he have a complete turn around? He had prayed the sinner's prayer with me as a child. Did he reaffirm that? Did he cry out to God, the week, or night before he died? I didn't know. (I still don't know.)

My anger toward God had softened through the years. I did not blame God for Jon's death. There were still lots of questions. My soul is not restored.

THERE IS NO MORE SECOND SON OF

A SECOND SON OF A SECOND SON.

PART THREE

UP OFF THE CANVAS

CHAPTER EIGHTEEN | ASHES

"THOUGH THE FIG TREE should not blossom, And there be no fruit on the vines, Though the yield of the olive oil should fail, And the fields produce no food, Though the flock should be cut off from the fold, and there be no cattle in the stalls. Yet I will exult in the Lord, I will rejoice in God my strength," Habakkuk 3:17-18.

Life seemed barren, at best. I was a long way from exultation or rejoicing. I did not know if I would ever get there.

From the ashes we can build a better day...
Justin Hayward

Even during the funeral, I thought there was some hope. Psalm 16:11 came to mind, "Thou wilt show me the path of life. In Thy presence is fulness of joy. In Thy right hand there are pleasures forever." God was saying, "I will teach you how to live, I will show you the path of life. From the depths of death, there will come life."

Patience has always been a problem. I was never that keen on waiting for the process to develop. I don't make New Year's resolutions. One year I made an attempt. I was going to try to be not so easily agitated. About mid-January I told Peggy about my resolution. She was not aware of it.

As a kid we used to sing an old hymn in church, called "I Will Praise Him." It was a mournful tune, not the kind of upbeat tempo that is usually associated with a song of praise. One of the verses says, "Though the way seemed straight and narrow, All I claimed was swept away. My ambitions, plans, and wishes, at my feet in ashes lay."

(And no, I did not have to look it up.) The writer was saying, "I was walking the straight and narrow way, (Jesus words for the path to heaven, Matthew 7:14, KJV.) and everything still fell apart." I could now relate, for more reasons than one.

I like to walk when I pray. I had already mapped out a 1.4 mile square route in the neighborhood. I took many trips, many laps, some days, more than one lap, even in the winter.

I cried out to God, sometimes literally. I poured out my heart. (Psalm 62:8) I asked my questions.

Crying out to God can not be underestimated. Scripture is filled with references to this, the Psalms in particular. Even if we are terrible, are far from God, we are still to cry out. See 2 Chronicles 2:16, through the rest of the chapter. See God's gracious response in 2 Chronicles 7:14.

If you are in danger, cry out to God. If you are in distress, cry out to God. If you need help, cry out to God. If you don't know what to do, cry out to God. You get the picture.

As an adult, I occasionally write songs. The first one I ever had copyrighted was music to Psalm 91:1. I don't sit down to methodically grind out music. It usually just happens, even unexpectedly, most of them when I am alone, walking.

During one of these walks I remember asking God for an income amount (among other things,) for our family. It was out of reach. It did not happen overnight, but
he met it. (Why was I so short sighted?)

About this time Josiah (was living out of state) began to encourage me with the verse, "Call to me, and I will answer you, and I will tell you great and mighty things, which you do not know," Jeremiah 33:3.

As an aside: For awhile, Josiah had the greatest message on his voicemail. It was, I am either away from my phone right now, or out of the country....This was actually true. One just never knew.

Somewhere in these walks a miracle began to happen. I was at least up off the canvas, still groggy, not sure what had hit me, or why. At least I was on my feet.

Along with the path of life, God put in my heart that he would be my "Restorer of paths to dwell in, Isaiah 58:12, KJV. It was not an audible voice. Again, It did not happen all at once, but I began to realize, God was putting the following in my heart:

"I WILL RESTORE YOUR SOUL"

It was a long path. There were a lot of boulders, and thick brush in the way. I did not know what it involved. There were requirements. I did not know what they were. The path can be different for everyone. During my walks, the following song was written: (In response to Jon's death)

POUR OUT MY HEART

You were there in the beginning, Abel, fell to the ground.
There has never been a time when you were not around.

You saw the pain and sadness in the eyes of
Adam and Eve.
And every man and woman since has needed to believe

That you are God. You are the great I AM.

And the harder things in life, are not greater than
Your love and your mercy, and all of your grace.
Who am I not to trust you, so I will take my place

With those who worship, With those who call
upon your name,
Whether from a heart of joy, or from a heart of pain.

You are God. You are the great I AM.
You are God, not man.

I will pour out my heart before you. I'll cry out
when I'm in need.
I will ask you all my questions. I will state my case
and plead.

It is for certain you have borne my griefs and
carried all my sorrow.
You give healing to the wounded heart and reason
for tomorrow.

You are God. You are the Great I AM.
And the harder things in life, are not greater than
Your love and your mercy, and all of your grace.
Who am I not to trust so - so I will take my place

With those who worship, With those who call upon
your name,
Whether from a heart of joy, or from a heart of pain.

You are God, you are the great I AM.
You are God, not man.

My thoughts began to turn to the possibility of what God could do, rather than what I had not done, what I had not been able to accomplish. God gave Adam a garden. He did not adequately protect it. Adam was a genius. He named all of the animals. I believe Adam's mind, before he sinned, and hid from God, was superior to anything we have seen since. I don't have book, chapter, or verse, for that.

I know science tells us we only use a small percentage of our brain. I believe Adam had full access to his. There is more to say about the mind, later in the book.

Adam had a garden. I had a son. I did not adequately protect my son. They made me caretaker of the vineyards, but I have not taken care of my own vineyard, Song of Solomon 1:6.

I, (we) tried to be very diligent in raising our children. All of my kids will tell you they were raised by two differences of parents. That happens in a lot of families. I had the same set of rules for all of them, but some of the personal freedoms and boundaries varied through the years.

We thought all of the kids would naturally follow the right path. We did not expect complete perfection, but almost. We gave it our best shot to be good parents.

I learned, way before Jon was any trouble that Christianity does not guarantee the following: Just because you are a Christian, does not mean you will be a good business man. If you learn, study, diligently apply the right principles, seek wisdom, are energetic, ambitious, and responsible, you have a great shot. On top of that, you will still need to ask God to bless you and give you favor. Just because you are a Christian, does not mean you will be good with money, even if you tithe. Tithing may be a preeminent prerequisite, but see the list in the previous paragraph.

For instance, I work diligently at my job, but there are some positions I would never qualify for, unless I seriously upped my computer skills.

You may not agree with me on the following: Just because it is mentioned in the Bible, does not mean it will automatically happen to you. The key word is, automatically.See "The Lord Is My Shepherd," and personal revelation, later in the book.

And so it was with me, with us, with Jon. It does take all of the parties involved, to bring about the will and the promises of God. This was a hard lesson. What we do with our life, even if others fail us, is critical.

About the same time as Pour Out Your Heart came to be, another song came during my walks. I wanted to hear from heaven. I wanted to hear what God had to say.

You understand, I am talking about what the Spirit of God communicates to our mind, our brain, to our human spirit. When I refer to the restoration of the soul, I'm talking in large part, about the condition of the human spirit.

The Bible says His Spirit will "Teach you all things," John 14:26. In this verse the Spirit of God is called the Comforter. Think about that. The New Testament Greek word means intercessor, consoler, advocate, comforter. Some Bible translations use the word Helper. I needed Someone to go to bat (advocate) for me, Someone with a better batting average than .143.

I needed all of the help and comfort I could get. And I certainly needed Someone to reteach me, or in some cases, teach me for the first time.

You already know how important music is to me. Years before, the idea about the "Music of Heaven" had come to me. Jesus' birth was announced in part by an angelic choir. I already knew they existed. I've already said, I believe all good music comes from heaven. (Every good and perfect gift comes from heaven (above), coming down from the Father....James1 1:17.

MUSIC OF HEAVEN

Oh Lord for today, I will hide away.
And I will cry out loud
As if there were a crowd

Oh Lord for today, I will hide away.
I want to hear your voice
Instead of all the noise.

I want to hear the singing
Of those who think they don't belong
When they realize that they can join the song.

I want the joy, of every girl and boy
Who left when they were young,
As their praise is sung.

Oh Lord for today, I will hide away.
And I will cry out loud
As if there were a crowd.

Oh Lord for today, I will hide away.
I want to hear your voice
Instead of all the noise.

The song of anticipation as you prepare for war
The sound of overcoming, death and sin will live no more.

The sounds of celebration that come from battles won.
A melody soft and sweet from those who hear you say well done.

Oh Lord for today, I will hide away.
And I will cry out loud
As if there were a crowd.

Oh Lord for today, I will hide away.
I want to hear your voice
Instead of all the noise.

I want to hear the crowns,
As they lay them down.

The music from the throne
Sung for you alone.

The sound of rushing waters, as from the Ancient of Days.
The song of all created things as they echo praise.

The voices lifted up in strength from those
no longer weak.
And the sound of silence, as You're about to speak.

Oh Lord for today, I will hide away.
And I will cry out loud
As if there were a crowd.

Oh Lord for today, I will hide away.
I want to hear your voice
Instead of all the noise.

CHAPTER NINETEEN | THE LOVE OF GOD

THE FOLLOWING CHAPTERS INCLUDE the things that were critical to me in the restoration of my soul.

Is it possible that this, "The Love Of God" is the least understood, the least experienced, and the greatest gift in the universe? Is it the most misinterpreted subject in the world? How many questions begin with, If God is a God of love, why....? If God is a God of love, how...? If God is a God of love, why doesn't He...? It makes a difference whether the question is asked by someone who is genuinely looking for truth, or by someone who hates God and is just looking for a fight. Both need an answer.

A famous theologian was asked, " What is the greatest truth in the Bible? I'm sure the questioner was looking for something profound, something deep. He got it. The reply was, "Jesus loves me, this I know, for the Bible tells me so."

It is not my purpose to answer all of these questions. Again, there are lots of books written by skilled people, that can help. I will simply use what God says about Himself, as a definition of His love. I need to take my definition of love and make sure it lines up with God's definition.

The Bible says "God is Love", 1 John 4:16. We know love by this, that He laid down His life for us.... : 1 John 3:16. And the Gospel of John, 3:16, "For God so loved the world that He gave....."But God demonstrates His own love toward us, in that while we were yet sinners, Christ died for us, Romans 5:8. See how great a love the Father has bestowed upon us, that we should be called the children of God, and such we are. 1st John 3:1.

Re: The rich young ruler, "Jesus beholding him, loved him. Mark 10:21 KJV.This young man was not a disciple. He was not going to become a disciple. Jesus knew that. He still loved him.

James and John were brothers and disciples. Jesus gave them a name which meant, Sons of Thunder, Mark 3:17. When I was in ministry prep, I wanted to be a Thunderer. That pretty well described the idea of the God of our youth. I don't think anyone actually said it, but the idea was, you were only one very minor slip up from the gates of hell. The subject of the love of God was pretty foreign, and greatly underplayed.

I never heard a sermon on the grace of God that was worth remembering or repeating, until we attended the church with the trumpet playing pastor. Ya gotta love those trumpeters. It was the major message of that church. They had a great understanding of grace.

I have neither the voice or the personality to be a Thunderer.

Even though we know about the love of God by definition, it is hard for many people, including Christians, to believe that God really does, genuinely, unconditionally, love them.

When I was an assistant at the church where I was so busy, my morning started off with dropping Sara at the church day care, and running Peggy to work. Sometimes I had just enough time to stop at a little restaurant counter, get a cup of coffee, a danish, and speed read the paper before running to the office. Life was frenetic. This little time alone got my day off to a good start.

One morning I vaguely noticed a man who sat across the counter from me. As I got up to leave he walked over and handed me a a fully opened white napkin. He had drawn my portrait, with great detail and accuracy. The first thing, and main thing I noticed were the sad eyes. I didn't realize.

To me, Steve Green's recording, titled "For God And God Alone" is one of the top three great recordings of all time. Read part of the following verse from cut number 8:

ONLY JESUS/CALVARY'S LOVE

(by Greg Nelson/ Phil McHugh)

Calvary's love can heal the spirit
Life has crushed and cast aside.
And redeem til heaven's promise
Fills with joy once empty eyes.

I think it captures at least part of the purpose of God's love. The love of God is so good, and powerful. God wants to say to your spirit, "I love you," with a depth and resonance that can change your life forever.

I owe some of the good that has come to my life over the last many years, to the International House of Prayer in Kansas City, (IHOP) to their founder Mike Bickle, and their entire staff. They have been helpful in defusing the idea of an angry God, just itching for an opportunity to smite his people for the slightest miscue. (That actually sounds more like my brothers and me as kids.)

Josiah introduced us to this ministry. They have had day and night, twenty-four hours a day, prayer and worship, non-stop, for twenty plus years. It is an amazing phenomenon. Along with other great ministries, they are changing the world.

I/we have gone down there many times. I have gone down there just to repent, and try to get my life on track when that was what I needed. On my first trip, my being was hit by the Presence of God before I took my second step inside their prayer room. Their worship teams have a leader, keyboard, guitars, a bass, drums, along with additional singers. Each team is "on" for two hours at a time. And they are very good.

I have been to their four-day, year end event called One Thing. The twins have been down there for One Thing. (down there, meaning south of Minneapolis.) When Erik writes his own book, he can tell you about his first invite to One Thing.

They have what I would call a modern "School of the Prophets." I met a man named Steve. He did not know me. The second thing he said was, "Write the Book." My response was, don't you mean "Write the Music?" His response was the same as at first. Write the book. So, this is the book.

Until then, writing a book was never a serious thought of mine. I do not know if it would have happened without him.

Anyway, God loves you. You can't deny it or change it. Why would you want to? God loves you. Enjoy it. Your sense of purpose, of acceptance, and value will increase when you recognize and really believe that He loves you. This was harder for me to accept than it should have been. It's one thing to know the words. It is another thing to have them resonate in your spirit as truth.

When Peggy and I decided we were on the same side, the same team, it made all of the difference in the world. When you find out that God is on your side, that He's not out to get you, it will make all the difference in your world.

When I make reference to "IHOP," or any other ministry, I don't pretend that I can accurately understand, articulate, summarize, or convey their teachings. I do my best to paraphrase with my limited analytical ability.

The following song falls in to the category of, they just don't make them like they used to.

OH LOVE OF GOD

Refrain by Frederick Lehman. 1917. Verse 3 (below) Unknown

Could we with ink the ocean fill,
And were the skies of parchment made,
Were every stalk on earth a quill,
And every man a scribe by trade:
To write the love of God above
Would drain the ocean dry:
Nor could the scroll contain the whole,
Though stretched from sky to sky.

Oh, love of God, how rich and pure!
How measureless and strong!
It shall forevermore endure
the saints and angels song.

CHAPTER TWENTY | I'M FORGIVEN

HOW DO WE RECONCILE EVENTS that appear to be bad, when the heart is good? Joseph, Job, and Daniel are some Scriptural examples of this. Joseph said of his brothers treachery, "You meant evil against me, but God meant it for good"...Genesis 50:20. Romans 8:28 says..."God causes all things to work together for good to those who love God, to those who are called according to His purpose."

No one has a perfect heart, but there are times in life, where it seems that things don't work out, even when our heart is pure. We ask, "Dear God, why isn't life going well, when I am doing well?"

I had to reestablish trust in God. I had to reestablish my faith that he was working for my overall good, whether or not I approved of all of life's current events. That took some time. I had to reestablish that whatever happened, my life was far better living with God, than if I was left to my own devices, without Him. I had to re-establish faith, or trust, in God, for the day-to-day and long term results of life.

God is always working, throughout the entire world, whether or not we think we see evidence of it. I am sure God was with me, even "carrying me," beyond the sight of the physical eye, when life was a struggle, and when I wondered if I was at least partially abandoned. I now know He was there.

The truth is, when we think God has forsaken us, God says, "I have inscribed you on the palms of my hands," Isaiah 49:16. "...I will never desert you, nor will I ever forsake you," Hebrews 13:5.

Beaten people many times reach a point where there is no emotion, maybe no ability to cry. The heart is hardened. They have nothing left in them to give. They might even lose the ability to care, or if they do, there is no ability or energy to do much about it. In worst case scenarios depression can take hold. All of this can change.

It's one thing to question life's outcomes when our heart is good. *What do we do if the heart is not good?*

We ask to be forgiven. This was a key step for me. On the cross, Jesus said, "Father, forgive them, for they do not know what they are doing," Luke 23:34.

What do we do if we know what we are doing is wrong, and we do it anyway? What if we are caught red handed? What if we know we are guilty? We ask for forgiveness. This was/is my problem. Anytime I do anything wrong, I know it is wrong.

I was raised in the church. I was raised on the Bible. I have known the difference between right and wrong my entire life. I have no excuse. Forgiveness is hard for me to accept.

There have been times where I almost felt hypocritical when asking for forgiveness. The wrong side of my mind would think, "C'mon, you did it on purpose. You knew what you're doing. Aren't you being more than a little presumptuous?

In one of my unfinished songs I write, " I wanted to to be Abraham, but lived too much like Lot. There is the contrast of Able vs. Cain, Jacob vs. Esau, David vs. Saul. Cain made bad choices and killed his brother Abel over his good choices. Jacob and Esau were separate for twenty years. Saul's choices, mainly of disobedience, cost him his throne and his life. They also cost him the life of his sons. Judas took his own life.

All of them could have been forgiven, including Judas. How do we know this? The Lord is....not willing for any to perish but for **all** to come to repentance, 2 Peter 3:9. Even David was angry at God, and lived to tell about it, 2 Samuel 6:8.

We talk about people who have heroes, Bible heroes, sports heroes, war heroes, and I guess, even political heroes. Do we ever think about God having a hero? Probably not.

However, consider David. He had supernatural encounters with God as a youth. God was there when he killed the lion and the bear, 1 Samuel 17:37. God was there when he killed Goliath, 1 Samuel 17:47. David was God's choice, (and he knew it) to be king over Israel, 1 Samuel 16:12. Multiple times David asked God if he should go in to battle. God answered him.

Later in life, David was where he was not supposed to be. (Who hasn't done that?) He was supposed to be at war, out on the battlefield with his army. He was not. He was home, up on his roof. (all of these roof top restaurants in today's society? David was way ahead of his time.)

We all know what happened. He had what we today would call an affair with the beautiful lady he saw from his rooftop. (The Bible does not say whether or not she was complicit.) To cover up the fact that she was pregnant, David brought her husband back from the war, but he did not go near his wife. David sent the husband back to the war, and gave orders to place him where death would be certain.

David then took the lady as his wife, one of many wives. God saw all of this. A prophet was sent to confront David. There were consequences. We know David repented, Psalm 51 is a record of his prayer. (Another part of my unfinished song, "Father, forgive me for I know what I have done. Father, forgive me, I have crucified the son…)

Even with all of this, David is promised by God, that his house, and kingdom and throne will be established forever. In Isaiah 9:7 the throne of Jesus is referred to as the eternal throne of David and his kingdom.

If David can be forgiven, you and I can be forgiven. We are never going to have a sense of freedom, or a spirit or soul that is free, if we carry around the guilt and weight of our past transgressions.

I have many unfinished songs. I have said for years that I want to be the "Colonel Sanders of Christian music". I think the Colonel started Kentucky Fried Chicken, (now Simply known as KFC) around the time of his retirement from his "Normal" job. I plan to be very busy when I retire. I have ideas for several more books. And the music won't wait. From:

THINGS I NEED TO SAY

David: I haven't met your measure,
God: Nor has anyone who's lived.
David: I've lost some of the treasure.
God: I know how to forgive.

This is the most important thing I have to say in the entire book. (No, you can't quit reading now.) God says, to you,

"I KNOW HOW TO FORGIVE."

"It's what I do. It's who I am. It's why I sent Jesus. God did not send Jesus to the cross, to die for the sins of the entire world, for everyone, just to back off and say, "Oh, I guess I changed my mind." ....For I, the Lord, do not change.... Malachi 3:8.

God does not have to have a round table discussion to decide whether or not He is going to forgive. He does not have to take several trips around the block, or around the lake to debate this issue with Himself. "For Thou, Lord, art good, and ready to forgive, and abundant in lovingkindness to all who call upon Thee." Psalm 86:5.

God has never failed in any of His attempts. In baseball, that would be batting 1000. The best any human has done "recently" was Ted Williams batting .406 in 1941, No, I did not have to look that one up either.

Consider Nehemiah 9:17, "But thou art a God ready to pardon, gracious and merciful, slow to anger, and of great kindness...." In the context of this verse, Nehemiah recalls a time where some of God's people were on their worst behavior. God was still ready to forgive.

God, really, is waiting to forgive. He wants to forgive. It's His nature. It's who He is. If your actions, or heart, or character have been worse than anyone can imagine, you can still be forgiven. You can be completely forgiven, with a clean slate. "...Though your sins are as scarlet, They will be white as snow," Isaiah 1:18.

CHAPTER TWENTY-ONE | I FORGIVE

FOR ME, THE LAST CHAPTER was easier than this one. But if you can make it through this subject, you might feel like you can win the whole battle.

Once we are forgiven by God, another side of forgiveness has to be addressed. In fact, in the Lord's Prayer we are told these two sides of forgiveness are inseparable, (Matthew 5:12). You may already be thinking, "Do I have to?"

In Matthew 18:23-35 we read of a slave who was shown forgiveness and mercy. His debt (literal in this case) was gargantuan. His debt was forgiven. Someone owed him a paltry sum. He would not forgive the debt. He would not reciprocate. The results were harsh. The "moral" of the story is, "We must forgive, from the heart," v35.

Matthew 6:14-15 says, "For if you forgive men for their transgressions, your heavenly Father will also forgive you. But if you do not forgive men, then your Father will not forgive your transgressions." There is no ambiguity in the statement.

How often have you heard someone say, "Well, I'll forgive, but I won't forget." I don't think that qualifies. I don't think it meets the criteria. I don't think that registers very high on the "from the heart'" scale.

I did not have a very long list of people on my anger sheet, that I kept in my head. But the ones who were there were entrenched. They were not easily released.

How often have you heard it said, "I have a right to be angry. You would be angry if the same thing happened to you. Or, you have no idea what they did, or how that affected me. They ruined my life." Have you made some of these statements?

We don't switch from anger, resentment, and unforgiveness overnight. We don't just wake up one day and say, "I'm all better now." We don't decide, just out of the blue, to bury the past.

For me, I did not want to forgive. I knew better, but that alone did not change how I felt and how I thought.

I am going to enter in to dangerous territory. I am going to talk about being a victim and having a victim mentality. In my head, I always fought against this idea. I did not like it.

Some times people are applauded for outrageous behavior, even terrible criminal activity because they are victims or were victims in the past. The thing about being a victim is, you may never be able to extract the type of response you think you deserve from the people who wronged you. We all know, terrible injustice has been inflicted upon people, throughout history, forever.

I do think God cares about social justice and social injustice. In making corrections, it is important that we do not do the right thing the wrong way.

For this book, my focus is on what happens to you and me as an individual. The principles apply to groups well.

When I saw the Henry Ford plaque, and was faced with the reality of my thought processes, I did not like what I saw in my mental mirror. I was, for the time, seeing myself as a victim. It took me a long time to make the needed changes.

I was blaming this person, and that person for some of the difficulty in my life. Even that made me mad, mad at myself. I had let people, people that I considered inferior to me (that wasn't right either, see Philippians 2:3) chart some of the course for my life. I've had a lot to work on.

I decided I would no longer look at life through the lens of being a victim. It's crippling. You can not change what happened in the past. **You can change where you are going to go in the future**. You do not have to see ourself as a victim going forward, regardless of the ancient, recent or current circumstances of your life. Some societies are fighting over issues that are hundreds and hundreds of years old.

Refusing to see yourself as a victim is **empowering.** It won't change generational inequities, but it can free you as an individual, to move forward and rise above them.

To be Forgiven, To Forgive, Combined with Personal Ownership of your Current State, and Future, is a Powerful Combination.

Who knows, if one "old man" in a gymnasium can single handedly change an entire atmosphere, a game, and a team's fortunes, what could happen through you to change your life, the life of a family, a company, a neighborhood, or more?

God's ability to work in your life, to help you, to restore you, is far greater that any past history, whether you are an individual, or part of a disenfranchised group.

I still was not willing to forgive. I had to refer to something I had done in the past. Because I knew forgiveness was the right, and necessary thing to do, I told God I was at least willing to be willing, to forgive. (If you can make it happen, let's see what happens.) He would have to help me, and soften my heart.

This began to happen slowly at first, very slowly. As it did I began to take responsibility. *You may never be able to accurately assess your level of responsibility for your role in "how you got to where you are."*

You can assume personal responsibility, for what you are going to do about it, and assume responsibility for where you are going to go in the future. Taking responsibility is a huge step in the forgiveness process, and a huge step in the soul restoration process. I did not need God to restore the soul of someone else, I needed Him to restore **my** soul. I needed to accept **responsibility for my life**, both past and present.

When I stand before God, no one else is going to be on the line, at that time. I am not going to give an account of what anyone else said, did, or thought. I will be giving an account for just me, of what **I** said, did, and thought. I will be the only one responsible then. I must be the only one responsible now.

Don Henley had a song called *"Heart Of The Matter"* written by Mike Campbell, Don Henley, and John David Souther. One line of the song says:

I think it's about forgiveness...Even if...

The song goes on to say, "I think it's about forgiveness, even if you don't love me any more." There are not many things tougher in life than a divorce/breakup. Forgiveness is offered, even if "I don't get the result I want." To me, this is profound.

I'm forgiving everything that forgiveness will allow...

This is a line from a Willie Nelson song, "*Nothing I Can Do About It Now*," written by Beth Neilson Chapman. There is a remarkable difference in the sentiment of the lines of the two songs. I think the second one is equally profound, just for different reasons.

I **can not go back and change anything that took place in the past, but I can choose how I respond to it.** I can make the right choices, no matter what anyone else has done in the past. I can not change the past, but **I can make the right decisions to give me a future that is better than the past. I can't change where I was, but I can change where I am going.**

What did I do? I asked God to help me change my attitude. He did. In restoring my soul, I really am talking about the Creator of the universe, speaking to us/me, putting thoughts, ideas, and attitudes in to our heart, mind, and spirit. We recognize a particular change or thought that happens, usually not all at once. It is a gradual, process, over a period of time, and we slowly recognize that a transformation has taken place.

Everyone has feelings. Everyone has disappointment. Everyone has tragedy. Everyone has been wronged, sometimes severely, more than should be humanly possible. I never want to trivialize the egregiousness of someone's situation or history. Atrocities do take place.

Some people just naturally seem to be like God, ready to forgive, easily, ready to move on, ready, willing, and able to forget. Others are like me, are able to remember names, dates and conversations, keeping mental lists. Every wrong was tabulated, cataloged, filed, and easily recalled.

The following starts a new subject, one that makes forgiveness difficult. Everyone has had to deal with someone we thought was unqualified. It can be a boss, a government employee, a court employee, a coworker. They make decisions that have significant impacts upon our lives. We wonder, how in the world did they get their job, or their position? And why are they still there?

But there they are, deciding what is going to be done and who is going to do it, who stays and who goes, who gets promoted and who doesn't.

I have worked for two major corporations that have a worldwide impact in their field. I have met and worked with what my daughter calls "wickedly brilliant people." In one company, until you got to know your way around, you never knew which of the people you met in the hallway had a PhD. I am just astounded at how many brilliant, gifted people there are.

Then you also see the other side of the coin. Not everyone fits in to the previous paragraph, and you wonder how the company ever gets anything done, or makes any money. Why do I bring this up? Because we need to forgive the people that we think make wrong decisions about our lives.

It's a whole 'nother story about the will of God not always being done, and people making wrong decisions. It happens. But I have to have enough faith in God that He will override bad decisions. Some times what we consider a bad decision, might be a disguised part of an ultimate plan for our good. We already talked about Joseph's "Path to Prime Minister."

Here is the second of one of the most important things I have to say:

GOD CAN TAKE US FROM WHERE WE ARE AND GET US TO WHERE WE NEED TO BE

Jesus was going to be crucified. It was going to happen. He was the "Lamb, slain from the foundation of the world," (Revelation 13:8 KJV.) "For this purpose I came to this hour, " (John 12:27.)

Caiaphas and Pilate were religious and civic/ government leaders at the time of Jesus' crucifixion. They ordered the crucifixion of Jesus. They killed the Son of God. That's not good. But there they were, stumbling, and bumbling along, making the most important decision in human history, and they had no idea what they were doing.

We all run in to Caiaphas and Pilate, usually several times in life. We can forgive them. Parents, spouses, children, bosses, neighbors, attackers, deserters, and thieves can be forgiven. (Even drivers and opposing sports teams can be forgiven, but that's pushing it.)

Here is one way to look at this subject. Our sin against God, our perfect Creator, is far greater that anyone's "sins" against us. If God is willing to forgive us for breaking His rules and commandments, we can forgive people for what are "comparative trivialities."

Every once in awhile, I would hear someone mention, in part of a sermon or a speech, or even in casual conversation, "Let it go, Get over it", "Move on, move up," etc. I would always think, "That's easy for you to say, you have no idea....etc." For some of you, offering ***forgiveness*** may be the ***most difficult thing*** you will ever do.

Tell God you are at least "willing to be willing." Tell Him you are at least willing to "enter in to negotiations." Tell Him you are at least willing to have exploratory conversations. *IF HE CAN MAKE IT HAPPEN, LET'S SEE WHAT HAPPENS.*

I no longer blame anyone, for anything. I refuse to say, "Well, I'd be in a better place, a better situation if so and so had not done such and such." I'm an adult, (finally.) I take full responsibility. No one is responsible for any thing in the past but me. No one is responsible for the course I take in the future, but me.

Sometimes you may be wronged/hurt/injured/wounded on purpose, with malice, with premeditation, kind of the opposite of a Caiaphas situation. It was done with intention, and meanness. This doesn't make it easy to forgive. Neither does it remove the need to forgive.

Can you be forgiven? Absolutely. For everything? Absolutely. Can you forgive? Absolutely. Everything? Absolutely.

What forgiveness is not: When you forgive, you are not saying that what the other person did was all right. You are not saying it didn't hurt, or that it didn't matter.

You **are** freeing them from future punishment, anger, and vengeance on your part. Jesus, in the Gospels, has a lot to say about how we should treat our enemies.

Did I forgive everyone? I did. Peggy and I have driven on some mountain roads that I consider scary; not wide, no guard rail in some places. They were also unmatched in beauty.

Forgiveness can help you get off the tortuous road, without guardrails. You may not be able to anticipate everything that is coming around the corner, but forgiveness is a critical step in the process of the beautiful life God has planned for us.

CHAPTER TWENTY-TWO | THE CARES OF LIFE

JESUS TAUGHT ABOUT HOW IMPORTANT it is to hear, understand, and "bear fruit" in regard to the Word of God. This parable is given in Matthew, Mark, and Luke. Jesus used the phrase "The Cares Of Life" to describe a process that inhibits us from maintaining followup on what we hear. Some translations use the phrase "the worries of the world" or the "worries of the age."

In life today, the pressure is on. The two companies I referenced earlier, both follow "Lean Manufacturing" principles, one of them on jet fuel. Lean Manufacturing is a term form the Toyota Manufacturing system. Two main books were written, The Toyota Way and the Toyota Way FieldBook, (Plus zillions of words related to the subject.) The term Lean Manufacturing means everything you probably think it means. Some companies swear by it. Some companies swear at it. Some companies do both at the same time.

Whether or not your company follows lean manufacturing or not, the pressure is on. Pressure to produce more, to cut costs, if need be to cut employees, to save space, to cut food costs, to cut labor costs, to produce more with less space, time, and money, to bill more hours, to cut energy costs, to cut carbon footprint, to produce more bushels per acre, yet use less chemicals.

If you run your own company, that is another complete different set of downs. No one is able to make comparisons to that unless they have tried it.

The pressure is on to put in more hours, to close the sale, to create more foot traffic, to finish the project on time and under budget, to look better, to think faster, to be more creative, to develop new products, and most of all, to beat the competition.

We haven't even touched on home life yet. There has to be time for the marriage, for the kids, for dental appointments, for the kids activities, to mow the lawn, to cook meals, to visit colleges, to do the car maintenance, to shop, to go to the doctor, to go to a ball game (of course,) to go to church, to work out, to sleep (?), to take care of aging parents, to maintain personal and professional relationships, to walk the dog, to do some kind community involvement, to keep up with the news. I'm exhausted.

And we wonder why medication use is up, why we can't sleep, why we are on edge, why we are tired, sometimes irritable, and out of patience and compassion. This was partly why I "encouraged" my kids to be a decent human being, to make good responses in the face of the challenges of life. Even at my lowest point, I did my best to be a decent human being, to not let my personal angst mar everything I touched or said.

Thoreau made a great analysis when he summarized, *"The mass of men live quiet lives of desperation."*

This is in part what Jesus was referring to, as, The Cares Of Life. There is a lot to do. The pressure is on us to do it all. Parts of society tell us we should want it all, we deserve it all, and we can have it all. A minister friend of the family, Pastor Londa, talks about getting off the crazy train.

Your heart, your motivation, your actions, and your relationships may all be in a great place and yet you may still be beaten, maybe not face down on the canvas, but beaten. Beaten because of The Cares Of Life. Life can wear you down, wear you out, even without some major calamity or miscue.

Even Jesus said, (…come away by yourselves to a lonely place and rest awhile." (Mark 6:31) Is it any wonder.

I told you earlier that the first instance of my interest in Peggy took place on the way to Denver. It was decades later, but we did get back there on a vacation. (Johnny River's song Summer Rain says, "She wants to live in the Rockies, she says that's where we'll find peace.") A long time ago I brought up the idea of living there. We never made it.

On our trip back to Colorado, we made it all the way to Moab, Utah. We fell in love with it, the mountains, the National Parks, the famous lodge and grounds where so many movies were filmed.

We loved it so much that we made a return trip three years later. While approaching Moab, we knew something was wrong with the car. Moab had the needed dealership. The car was still under warranty. We weren't expecting any trouble. This was on a Friday. The needed part would not arrive until Monday. It was Tuesday before installation was complete. I would not call Moab a lonely place, but we cooled our jets, and rested awhile. It was very relaxing.

There was a time where that scenario would have caused me lots of weeping and wailing and gnashing of teeth.

At the time I still had an old flip phone. It met my needs. (I hear they are coming back in style.) Peggy is more up to date. While we were without wheels, we found very good accommodations with a pool. It was summer and sunny. Several restaurants were within walking distance.

I asked Peggy to look up some old music on her phone, music I had almost

forgotten. I sat by the pool, earphones in, listening to Chuck Girard's songs "Slow Down" and "Lay Your Burden Down." "Lay our burden down, get your feet on solid ground." Good music never gets old, the right song at the right time.

God does that for us. He has just the right word at the right time. I've told you about working overnights. One night I was working in an area where there were just two of us. The other gentleman was a young man from another country…He had his Christian worship music coming from a speaker. He knew I approved of his playlist. Some of it was in his language, not mine. I told him I appreciated the music, that it touched my heart. I could "understand" even the words I could not translate.
God's "message" may come to us from anyone, anywhere, any time. Several times I have used the phrase in this book, "I was just sitting there, minding my own business, and God…… It is usually when I don't expect it.

Businesses take inventory, for all of the reasons we would Imagine. We need to take inventory as well, not just to annually check our health or our portfolio.

Am I on the right track? Am I going in the right direction? Is this what I/we want? Do we need to make adjustments? Sometimes we have to make hard choices. Sometimes it seems we have to choose between the better of two evils while we are on our journey to being able to choose between better and best. Do we need to make a move, to a new neighborhood, school, city, or job?

There is a radio show in the Twin Cities. Part of the show has talked about a man's value being directly related to how many cylinders he owns. I never did call in to tell the host about my dad.

Another part of the show talks about not sitting in traffic. If it's a Friday, and a road is jammed with traffic, the host will call it "Make a move Friday." He doesn't believe in sitting in traffic, waiting for something to happen. "Find a different road, take a side street, keep moving." The Cares Of Life don't allow you to waste all of your time in traffic.

One man on the West coast tied helium balloons to his lawn chair, strapped himself in, cut loose the lawn chair, and off he flew. He caused problems with airplane's flight paths. When asked why, he replied, "Sometimes you just can't sit there." I think he meant, doing nothing.

I love the message of the church we attend. If I understand it correctly, one of the phrases is, "Anything is possible."

That phrase "Anything is possible," grips me. When you've "lost your soul," whether it's from your mistakes or just from the pressure of The Cares Of Life, you don't believe much is possible, at all. Your faith, whatever is left of it, is at low tide. It's gone out to sea. It's hard to believe anything will ever be any different.

There was a time where we wondered if our marriage could be any better. When I was at the "End Of The Line" chapter, I could not imagine the wonderful life we are now allowed to live.

It is time to believe, or believe again, "Anything is possible." It may take some time. Start to believe that life can be different, any area of life. It might be time to make a move. Sometimes you just need to take one step. (See Joshua 4:14.)

I said that I would mention faith and the faith message. As with grace, and with the faith message, there has been some nonsense in some places.

I went to a "Faith Church" for a year. The things they were accused of saying, they didn't say. The things they were accused of teaching, they did not teach. The worship was great, the messages varied, and inspiring.

I want to hear a message of hope, a message about how Great God is, about how Powerful He is, about how much He Loves me, about Divine Intervention, about the Goodness of God, about His Ability to Accomplish His Purposes in My Life and in His World.

In John, chapter eleven, Lazarus has died. Disciple Thomas suggested that they all go die with him. This is not what I want to hear when I go to church.

Jesus raised Lazarus from the dead. Talk about "Getting Up Off The Canvas!" Here's something about faith. Jesus "marveled" twice in Scripture. In Matthew 8:6, He marveled at the centurion's great faith, "I have not found such great faith with anyone in Israel." The centurion's faith was rewarded. His servant was healed.

Mark 6:6 says of Jesus, "And He marveled because of their unbelief." Verse 5a says, "And He could do no miracle there." (KJV) I'm sure many have used this phrase: I would rather have God marvel at my faith, than marvel at my unbelief.

If you are using your faith **only** to amass material possessions, you'll be disappointed. If faith is applied to all of life, and the advancement of "the Kingdom," that's good.

It's far better to surround yourself with people who believe in the goodness and the power of God, than it is with people who say, you might as well curl up and die.

You can't change where you have been, but can change where you are, and where you are going. God may want to tweak your life. He may want to reinvent your life. What I saw as "The end of my world" in the "End of the Line" chapter, turned out to be the beginning of a new life.

It did not end my ability to have an impact on the lives of people. It would take place in a different form. This book is yet another different form.

The cares of life will continue to pull at you. Proverbs 4:23, "Keep thy heart with all diligence, for out of it are the issues of life," KJV.

I loved this song, long before I thought my life had fallen apart:

HE GIVETH MORE GRACE. By Annie J. Flint

He giveth more grace when the burdens grow greater.
He sendeth more strength when the labors increase.
To added afflictions He addeth His mercy.
To multiplied trials, His multiplied peace.

His love has no limits, His grace has no measure.
His power has no boundary known unto men.

For out of his infinite riches in Jesus
He giveth, and giveth, and giveth again.

When we have exhausted our store of endurance,
When our strength has failed ere the day is half done,
When we reach the end of our hoarded resources,
Our Father's full giving as only begun.

His love has no limits, His grace has no measure.
His power no boundary known unto men.
For out of His infinite riches in Jesus
He giveth, and giveth, and giveth again.

People come in and out of our lives at different times. I used to spend some time with a man who was full of faith. He talked about it, a lot. It was important to him. He was fully convinced about Fatih's place in life.

I caught up with him some years later and asked how he was doing, in relation to faith. His response was, I"m just a man trying to make a mortgage." I don't think he was despondent or "Down in the Pit." My interpretation of his response was, "The Cares Of Life" had taken some of his edge. He was still in the ring, still standing, still fighting, but too tired to throw very many punches. At the time he said this, I was still somewhat in the same place. I was in the process of having my soul restored, but not far enough along to offer much help or enthusiasm.

One of the keys to Restoring your Soul, and not falling in to the Pit, is winning the battle in "The Cares of Life." Have the discussions with the important people in your life. For Peggy and I, each of our recent housing transitions have included serious downsizing. We even rented some storage space for a time, while we decided what to do with some of our stuff.

We have a lot of "Stuff" in life, whether it is actual possessions, or the "Stuff" of schedule. Is downsizing your "Stuff" on your schedule?

Later in the book there is the phrase, "Make a List." This is something we can do with "The Cares Of Life." Make a list of all of the important things in your life, prioritize them. Your initial list may be very long.

In your list, make one section with the heading, "Non Negotiable," meaning, the things on this part of the list are essential, non debatable items, as in "I must do them, I must have them". The middle section can be what we have always considered life's other necessities. These may need to be reassessed, reprioritized, or in some cases, even dropped. The last part of our list can include "as time and circumstances allow."

I am not suggesting that you "drop out" and enter some counter culture life, but we may, at times, need to make what at first, seem like drastic changes, to "get our life back on track and get our ducks in a row."

CHAPTER TWENTY-THREE | IN ONE PIECE

MY KIDS KNOW, and most everyone else, knows the greeting I will give them, and a question I will probably ask, if we end up with time, for any type of discussion. I ask them if they are alive and well. They can give any kind of short or long answer They want to.

I ask them if they know anything. They can give as much or as little news as they want to. With Sara, we usually get news on a little bit of a delay, but then once we see her, the term she uses is "fire hose." An hour or two can pass while we are brought up to date, and she sometimes apologizes for fire hosing us.

Josiah is usually an open book. Erik is more open on a one-on-one basis. He is thoughtful, and chooses his words carefully. Elijah tends to hold things "close to the vest." His day is coming.

When I ask them if they know anything, they know I am not only asking about what they know, I am also asking, "Is there anything I need to know?" Is there anything you want me to know?

When the twins were about thirteen years old, all four boys were together one day. I told them that there were four boys in my family. The youngest is the most like his dad. I could see the color drain from Elijah's face as I asked the question, "What if the youngest boy in our family were the most like his dad?"

Tell me about what you are doing...

Moody Blues drummer Graeme Edge in his song, *"I'll Be Level With You,"* makes this request of his son, "'I'll be level with you, The one thing I hope you will do, Is to tell me about what you're doing from time to time." Isn't That the request of every parent?

I am very fortunate to have access to my kids, when they are in the country. The other question I ask, is, "**Are You In One Piece?"** They know what I mean by that.

The deepest core of the question could be translated, "How is your soul? Is it restored, or shattered? What direction is your life going? Are you falling apart, on the mend, or doing great? Are you having a good day, or a good life? Are you having just a bad day, or a bad life?" Long before I ask the question I have looked in to their eyes to try to make a mini assertation.

My kids don't owe me a detailed expose, or a detailed explanation of any part of their life. They do know I care, and I am grateful to be included in their overall life. Peggy and I purposefully, and carefully, raised our kids with the goal of having a great relationship with them when they were adults.

Even on short phone conversations, I will ask Peggy, what do you know, or simply, is there anything I need to know? (I had better know if she is in one piece, without asking.)

God does care about every detail of our life, to the point that every hair on our head is counted, Matthew 10:30. He knows about every detail of our life. Jesus shocked Nathaniel when He said, "When you were under the fig tree, I saw you." John 1:48.

Hagar, was not "In One Piece." She was a recent outcast from her family. She was with her son in the wilderness, and literally, sat down to die. God sent an angel from heaven, with provision and instruction, and the promise of a future. This story is in Genesis chapter 21.

I have an untold number of favorite songs. One of them is an old song from a group called The Gamble Folk. The song is "*Sold For A Farthing.*" The words are almost a quotation of the story Jesus told about two sparrows.

There is a key Scripture, a promise that helped me recover. It was critical in the restoration process. I mean, exactly how does God take the terrible things, the pain, the brokenness of our lives, even the anger and resentment, despair, and hopelessness, and turn us into one piece, restored, and full of life?

Isaiah 53:4 says, "**Surely** our griefs He Himself bore, and he carried our sorrows. In the same setting, verse 5 says, "He was pierced through for our transgressions, He was crushed of our iniquities...."

Jesus came, not just so we would be forgiven, which in itself is really good, but also so he could remove the grief and sorrow from our lives. He bears our grief, and carries our sorrow, so we don't have to drag them along.

Jesus said, "Come to me, all who are weary and heavy laden, and I will give you Rest...And you shall find rest for your souls," Matthew 11:28-29.

Let's look at some more good news: The Gospel is good news: "For behold I bring you good news of a great joy which shall be for all the people," Luke 2:10. Isaiah 51:11, "They will obtain gladness and joy, And sorrow and mourning shall flee away."

Isaiah prophesied about Jesus in chapter 61. Jesus confirmed the prophesy in Luke 4. Isiah 61:1, "He hath sent me to bind up the broken hearted... (One meaning of the word bind, is to heal") v2, To comfort all who mourn, v3 To grant those who mourn in Zion, Giving them a garland (beauty) instead of ashes, The oil of gladness instead of mourning, The mantle of praise instead of fainting…"

Think about the card with the broken heart from an early chapter. God would ask you, "Does this belong to you? If it does, can I have it?" All of the promises of these verses are available for us, and more. In sports, teams trade players to other teams. They hope that someone they really don't want, can be traded for someone they think can help the team in the future. All of these exchanges above, sound like great trades.

Just as surely as Jesus died for our sins, He (Himself) bears our griefs, and carries our sorrows. Our sin was transferred to Him, forgiven, and forgotten,…I will forgive their iniquity, and their sin I will remember no more, Jeremiah 31:34) Jesus bears our griefs and carries our sorrow, so we can forget them.

You go to the dentist to get a tooth extracted. You go to God to get the pain in your life extracted. God will reach in to the extreme, very depth of your soul, in your deepest places, even the ones you hide from everyone. He will extract the pain, the grief, the sorrow, the anger.

God Himself, The Spirit of God, The Comforter, the Helper, puts thoughts, ideas, and instructions in our mind, His Spirit puts hope, healing, and life in our Soul. His Spirit even helps us pray, "…helps our weakness, for we do not know how to pray as we should, but the Spirit himself intercedes for us with groaning too deep for words," Romans 8:26.

A doctor removes a cancerous tumor. God removes what eats at our soul.A doctor resets a broken bone. God resets a broken life. Are you "In One Piece?"

This is literally a miracle that God will do for you. No human can do this for you. At some point, it's just you, "Crying Out To God," (more on this later) and God speaking back to you.

GOD'S PRESENCE HEALS

No one else may know who you are, what you've done, what you wanted, the secrets of your soul, or the depth of what you need, but God does. God can take the cold heart, the hard baked, bitter, angry, defeated, nailed shut, padlocked, fortress of a heart, soften it, and heal it, with the presence of the Holy Spirit.

This is not a self help book. It is important that we think correctly, but the issues I am talking about can not be overcome by correct thinking only. "David encouraged himself in the Lord," 11 Samuel 30:6 KJV.

When our lives appear like Humpty Dumpty after the fall, it takes more than mental consent to put our lives back together. Only God can do that. Just like our lives are worth more that sparrows, when God reassembles Humpty Dumpty, (without the scars) it is more beautiful, and worth more that the finest Faberge Egg. Can it really happen? Yes

God wants to help you. You will never be good enough to earn His help, attention, or grace. No amount of penance, giving, or good deeds will qualify you for assistance. You don't have to be perfect, or have it all figured out.

YOU DON'T HAVE TO BE A CHRISTIAN TO RECEIVE HELP FROM GOD

I'm not even sorry if that sounds like a heretical statement. It's true. (The rain falls on the just and the unjust.) Hear me out. Two main examples are given in Scripture:

Jesus called sinners to be disciples. Most of them were rough characters. They were neither the respected or elite of society. Matthew is the chief poster child. He was a tax collector, despised by everyone but the Roman authorities. The religious elite were aghast that Jesus would even associate with these people.

Once Jesus called them, they did not automatically, overnight, become paragons of piety. (I don't know that they ever became paragons of piety.)They were a work in progress. Some of their mistakes are clearly spelled out in Scripture. Yet they did the works of the Kingdom. Jesus called them. The needed work took place over time. Eventually they changed the world.

Jesus did two main things while he walked the earth. He taught the good news of the Gospel, the Kingdom of heaven, and He healed people. Matthew 8:16 and 12:15 are just two references that say, "He healed them all." He healed the good and the bad. He healed the just and the unjust. He healed the righteous and the reprobate.

He did not stop to question each one. Can you imagine how much time that would have taken? There were no forms in triplicate to fill out ("Have you broken any commandments this week?" If so, state which ones, how often, and what remedial steps you will take so it does not happen again?)

The sick are not greeted with, "Have you been to church this week? Have you paid your tithe? Are you one of my disciples? Have you thought ill of your neighbor or the boss". That could disqualify half the population right there.

He healed them all. He healed them all.
He healed them all.

Mathew 9:36, "And seeing the multitudes, He felt compassion for them, because they were distressed (harassed) and downcast like sheep without a shepherd."

Matthew 14:14, "And when he went ashore, He saw a great multitude, and felt compassion for them, and healed their sick." God has compassion for you - To heal you - To restore your soul - To resurrect your life.

Luke 19:41, And when he approached , He saw the city (Jerusalem) and wept over it." This is our God.

Most people who hear the word of God, and are miraculously healed are going to want to know more about this God. It was a "chance" Jesus was willing to take.

(I think God weeps over Detroit. I think God weeps over Cleveland. I think God weeps over San Francisco. I think he weeps over our American cities. (And of course, not just the cities of our nation.)

I have not touched on the following subject yet. There are multiple reasons to have our soul restored. There are many reasons we need to be "In One Piece." One is because of the compassion and goodness of God.

The other is "There is work to do." If we go back to Isaiah 61 and pick up right where we left off, v3 ends with the reason for our "restoration"...v4, "So they will be called oaks of righteousness, The planting of the Lord, that He may be glorified. They will rebuild the ancient ruins. They will raise up former devastations, And they will repair the ruined cities.

Minneapolis is a beautiful city. It (means) a city of lakes. In the early seventies there was still a law on the books that said no building could be taller than the twenty-nine story Foshay Tower. That was a problem for the fifty-seven story, soon to be, IDS Center. It was built. It is the site of the opening credits of the old Mary Tyler Moore Show. It is a magnificent building, and helped spark a renaissance of development. The downtown I knew in college is unrecognizable today.

In December of last year I read that Detroit is getting some major new sky scrapers in the near future. That's great. I am sure it will help. Buildings may be part of the physical glory of a city, but the people and the neighborhoods are the soul. Our collective soul needs restoration.

God said to Cain, " The voice of your brother's (Abel) blood is crying to me from the ground." (You don't think God weeps over our cities ?)

This is the beginning of a long story. Peggy and I took a vacation to San Diego to celebrate another milestone anniversary. (Recently I said to her, "You know, we are a lot closer to "happily ever after" than we used to be.")

We had not been back long when we got a call from Josiah. He told us about "The Call." It is an organization, started by Lou Engle. We first heard of him through Kansas City. There was going to be a 24 Hour "Call" in Sacramento. The purpose for these meetings is to pray for the city, also the state. Did we think we could/should attend? We decided to go. We arrived more than a day early. Peggy and I took a day to go to Lake Tahoe. It was one of the most enjoyable days of our life. We were blown away by the beauty and spent as much time there as we could.

The next day we walked through the capitol building in Sacramento. Arnold Schwarzenegger was still governor. A tour was in process for some young children. We walked in behind them. There was a statue of a bear outside the governor's office. The tour guide could not hide her joy that the governor would be leaving next year, and taking his bear with him.

Opening night of The Call was held in the Sacramento Bees minor league stadium. The next day everything was in front of the Capitol, with the crowd filling in the lawn and down the streets toward the river. There was worship. There were speakers. There was prayer.

We got to go to San Francisco for a couple of days. Josiah joined us. It was a good trip, very worthwhile. "The Call" was worth the trip, even if we had been unable to do any sightseeing.

Many things stand out about that trip. One is, if you are facing the capitol, standing maybe a block or two, to the west, there is a building on your left. The inscription at the top of the building reads:

"GIVE ME MEN TO MATCH MY MOUNTAINS."

Nothing more needs to be said.

A year later "The Call" was held in Detroit. I helped drive one of two church vans (through the night of course.) It was good, but it was a "tougher" meeting than the one in Sacramento.

Native Americans were given the first hours. If gave us a chance to acknowledge and appreciate their history in the city. During most of the rest of the meeting, many bishops from Detroit and some from other cities spoke. They brought clarity to the spiritual, cultural, social, and moral dilemmas past and present. We were challenged by some of the grim details of what has happened to the soul of the city. There is a lot of work to be done.

Dear God, what men and women, (including the very young) whose souls have been restored, are You calling to help restore the cities (and rural areas) of our nation? Give us men and women to match the mountain. As you pray, as you "Cry Out To God," He will replace brokenness, with wholeness; hopelessness, with fulfillment; anger, with forgiveness; grief, sorrow, ashes, and mourning, with comfort, beauty and joy.

I pray that you will realize God's help to put your life back together, that you will be "In One Piece." I pray the same for our nation and its cities.

PART FOUR

THE PATH OF LIFE

CHAPTER TWENTY-FOUR| THE PATH OF LIFE

DAVID IS WATCHING HIS FATHER'S SHEEP. He is their shepherd. I almost wonder if he was exiled to the job by the seven older brothers. What little is said about the family interaction leads us to believe there was not much respect or appreciation for him.

Samuel came to Jesse's house to anoint one of his sons to be the next king of Israel. He wanted to know if Jesse had any more sons, more than the seven who were present. I paraphrase 1 Samuel 16:11, "Yeah, there's one more, the youngest. He's out with the sheep." In 1 Samuel 17:28 it is very clear that David's oldest brother disdained him.

While David is alone, apart from human contact, it is clear that God is talking to him, (to his heart, to his consciousness, to his mind). David knows he is the Shepherd of the sheep. At some point, God tells him. **"I AM YOUR SHEPHERD."** Killing a lion and a bear might help drive that point home.

David later writes "The Lord is **MY** Shepherd." This may sound simplistic, but it was Divine Revelation, to a young lad, I am **their** shepherd, the Lord is **my** shepherd. It would serve him well for decades to come.

He escaped the individual attacks of King Saul. He escaped the murderous pursuit of Saul's army. He met Goliath in the valley of the shadow of death. He faced the armies of the Philistines, and multiple other armies during his reign as king over Israel.

All of us need this. We need God to make His promises real to us on a personal basis. There is difference between Scripture just "being there," and owning it.

I remember buying our first new car. There was a program where we could get a new car at cost. We went, planning to buy the cheapest new car they had. The selection for this program was not huge. We were not sure what to do. We looked at a model that was more expensive than our original plan. We talked. We hemmed and hawed. We were indecisive. We went to a restaurant to talk, to lay out the pros and cons. Should we or shouldn't we? We did. The car was stunning. It was powerful.

If we had not made an investment in that car, it would have just sat there on the showroom floor. We had to make it ours. Many years later, after our car was long gone, a man in our church drove the same, year, make, and model car on to the church parking lot. I offered him a profit on the spot.

Scripture is the same way. We don't have to buy it, but we have to own it, rather than it just sitting there. God has to make it real to us, to put it in our hearts to make it personal. His Spirit does this for us. God made the promise of the Shepherd real, and personal, to David. *HE MADE THE PROMISE OF RESTORATION REAL TO* ME.

One day Jesus was talking to a crowd. His words were difficult to hear, not because Jesus did not speak loud enough, but because of the meaning of His words. Some people left. They were unwilling to receive the message. Jesus turned to the disciples and said, "Do you want to go away also, Do you?" (John 6:67) Peter answered, "Lord, to whom shall we go? You have words of eternal life." (John 6:68)

Earlier in John 6:63 Jesus told them..."The words that I have spoken to you are spirit and life. God wants to show you "The Path Of Life." God has a good life planned for you. Even if you have had massive failures in the past. Even if you have sinned, greatly, in the past. Even if you did the sin on purpose. You may have gone through life (so far) in a fog, not giving much thought to anything, with no great plan or structure. God has a good life planned for you.

In John 10:10 Jesus said, "I came that they might have life, and might have it abundantly." This verse is an open window to the heart of God. Life will have its difficulties. Jesus confirmed this. He said, ..." In the world you have tribulation, but take courage; I have overcome the world." John 16:33. The third major thing I want to communicate to you, in the whole book is this.

God says:

I AM BIG ENOUGH TO FIND A

WAY FOR YOU TO PLEASE ME

You may have chosen the path of destruction. God will show you The Path Of Life. You may have chosen a path of willful disobedience.

HE KNOWS HOW TO FORGIVE
HE KNOWS HOW TO GET YOU FROM WHERE YOU ARE TO
WHERE YOU NEED TO BE
HE IS BIG ENOUGH TO FIND A WAY
FOR YOU TO PLEASE HIM

These are the reasons this book was written. This is the reason I told my story.

This was a real struggle for me. I was no wins and all losses for everything. (It did seem that way to me.) And this happened while I was trying to "please Him." Believing that it would be possible for me to please God in the future was a real stretch.

God will show you The Path Of Life. This became very real to me in the valley of death. It was not just the valley of the shadow of death. It was the actual valley of death. It was here, that I sensed God saying to my heart, "I will show you The Path of Life."

You have not burned all of your bridges. You have not burned all of your bridges with God.

GOD WILL MEET YOU WHERE YOU ARE SO

YOU DO NOT HAVE TO STAY WHERE YOU ARE

He will show you The Path Of Life.

In the introduction I encouraged you to read the book, because I know how to get out of the pit. I knew how to get up off the canvas.

The following chapters are the steps I would recommend, to move away from a broken, down for the count, face down on the canvas, shattered soul condition. The end of Romans 6, verse 4 says, "walk in newness of life."

Some people go to the stock car races just to see the crashes. Some people go to the hockey games just to see the fights. I've talked enough about crashes and fights. Let's see if there is more to life.

CHAPTER TWENTY-FIVE | HEAR THE WORD OF THE LORD

NUMBER ONE:

The first thing we need is to ***HEAR THE WORD OF THE LORD.***

A doctor resets broken bones. That is not a new concept to God. Ezekiel was taken to the valley of dry bones, very dry bones. They were dead. In Chapter 37, God challenged him, and asked, "Son of man, can these bones live?" (v3.) Ezekiel was told to prophesy over the bones, to say to them, "Oh dry bones, Hear the Word of the Lord…I will cause breath to enter you that you many come to life, (v4-5.)

It gets even stronger. "I will open your graves and cause you to come up out of your graves," (v12.) "I will put My Spirit within you, and you will come to life," (v14.)

Nothing will bring attention more than the dead coming to life. The dead bones had to hear the Word of the Lord if they were going to live, if they were going the be resurrected. (Ezekiel 37:4)

If your defeated spirit is going to live, it has to Hear the Word of the Lord. If your discouraged soul is going to be restored, it has to Hear the Word of the Lord. If you are going to be able to get up off the canvas and walk on the Path of Life, you need to Hear the Word of the Lord. If your emotions are numb to the point that you don't even care, and can't even cry, they need to Hear the Word of the Lord. If your situation is desperate and you don't know what to do, you need to Hear the Word of the Lord. There is no replacement.

In John 7:46 it is said of Jesus, "Never did a man speak the way this man speaks." I go to a church where I can't wait to hear what the minister has to say. (and I am not easily impressed.) I know I will Hear the Word of the Lord. Sometimes the Word of the Lord will surprise us. It will not always be what we expect. "I was just sitting there, minding my own business..."

The Word of the Lord is the Bible. It simply is. I offer that without apology. (This is not an apologetics book. There are lots of those.) Read the Bible. Study the Bible. Pray the Bible. Memorize the Bible. Sing the Bible. Speak the Bible.

Sometimes when you read, certain verses will mean something special to you. God will make them "yours." At times I have kept a record of the things that seem important to me as I read them. I have one Bible that is all marked up, underlined, underlined in red. When I started reading the Bible as if I were reading it for the first time, I got a different Bible, and did not make any notations or lines.

Some times the Word of the Lord comes through people. He may send a man to you to tell you to write a book. My thought along with the music question was, "a book about what?"

Find people who will encourage you and speak life in to you. Find people you know you can trust.

Over a period of time you will begin to know that God is speaking to you, that He is helping you, that He is with you, and that he is making a difference.

Some of the disciples had fished all night, and "caught no fishes." Jesus told them to go out again, to let down their nets.The Word of the Lord was spoken to them.

Then their boat was "full of fishes," Luke 5:4-6. (From one of the "motions" songs of my youth.)

The Bible is written. We can not add to Scripture. But God is still talking, making Scripture known to us, telling us how to apply Scripture. In fact, Amos 3:7 says, "Surely the Lord does nothing unless He reveals his secret counsel to His servants the prophets."

Joel 2:28 and Acts Chapter 2 speak of God pouring out His Spirit upon all flesh, complete with prophesy, dreams, and visions.

Do we think in the following terms? There is only one God. He has only one voice. The same God who spoke to the writers of the Bible is the same God who speaks to your mind. The same inner voice they heard when they put quill to parchment, is the same voice that speaks life to your soul. Hear The Word Of The Lord!

You may ask, "What if I knew what to do and did not do it? What if I did not follow the Word Of The Lord?" Peter denied Jesus three times. He was not kicked out of the Kingdom. In fact, a special invitation is made to Peter to let him know he was included in the future, Mark 16:7.

It is said of Jonah, the unwilling prophet, "Now the Word Of The Lord came to Jonah the second time... Jonah 3:1. Nothing will make a greater difference in your life than Hearing The Word Of The Lord.

CHAPTER TWENTY-SIX | CRY OUT TO GOD

NUMBER 2:
CRY OUT TO GOD

Pour out your heart before him, (Psalm 62:8) your whole heart. He can take it. I love Psalm 116:1-2. "I love the Lord, because he hears my voice and my supplications. Because He has inclined His ear to me, Therefore I shall call upon Him as long as I live." The context is one of terror, distress, and sorrow, v3. Psalm 34:6, "This poor (afflicted) man cried and the Lord heard him, and saved him out of all his troubles."

In the beginning these cries don't need to be lengthy or poetic. We don't have to form our words in iambic pentameter. We don't have to use the most proper form of the king's English.

Side Note: The show is about to start. There is a well dressed man in the audience, but he is kind of resting on a couple of chairs. An usher tells him he'll have to sit up straight. The show is sold out. The man doesn't move. He says nothing. Finally, a police officer is called to encourage the man's cooperation. One of the questions the officer asks is, "Hey buddy, where you from? The man leans up on one elbow, points up with his other hand, and in a weak voice, says, "Balcony." Some times when you're really hurting, you don't have a lot to say.

God can understand a simple cry of "Help." Is anybody out there? God, are you there? I need you. Pull me out of the pit."

Soon you will start to get more specific. Tell God where you are, what's going on,what you want, what you need Him to do. Ask your questions.

God came to Adam and Eve in the garden in the cool of the day. Genesis 3: 8 says, " they heard the sound of the Lord God walking in the garden in the cool of the day." They recognized the sound of the footsteps of God. The fact that they recognized His footsteps tells us this was a normal thing, God coming to talk to them.

The astounding thing about this verse is, this was after Adam and Eve sinned.

They had ruined their lives and destroyed civilization, but God came to talk to them. They had to start over. God helped them.

You may think you, or someone else has destroyed your life. I like the idea of a line from the movie, The Best Marigold Hotel. The main character says, "In my country we have a saying: "Everything will be all right in the end. If everything is not all right, it is not the end." There is not a chapter and verse for that, but you get the idea. If you are alive, it is not the end.

In general terms, there are two themes in the Psalms. One theme is crying out to God, "I'm in trouble, distress, I"m about to go under." The other theme is one of praise, for what God has done, for what He is doing, and for what He will do. The two themes are related.

As your "Hear The Word Of The Lord, and as you Cry Out To God, He will begin to speak to your heart, your mind, your spirit. He will encourage you. Faith will begin to take root. Scripture verses will turn in to promises. God will start to bring them to reality.

When I use the term "Cry Out To God," I am partly referring to what is commonly called prayer. The word "prayer" can be a generic term to convey everything from "Bless This Food", to "Save My Life."

Crying Out To God, is a part of prayer. I use it to denote a level of intensity and seriousness. Of course prayer, and all of what that term implies, is important to the restoration of the soul.

More than once, God has brought almost immediate help to my situation when I Cried Out To Him. This term implies more that the generic, more than a repetitious prayer, uttered without thought, more than a "now I lay me down to sleep" prayer.

It does not imply begging. We are the King's sons and daughters. ..."For your Father has chosen gladly to give you the kingdom. Luke 12:32.

In the phrase, Crying Out To God, I am not implying that He is deaf, or not listening. Rather, I am encouraging you to tell God everything, with full feeling and emotion. Life has critical moments. God is there, in them, even if you don't always sense or see His hand at work in your situation. Cry Out To Him. He will not hide.

CHAPTER TWENTY-SEVEN | WORSHIP

NUMBER 3:
WORSHIP

When unspeakable tragedy struck, Job bowed and worshipped. I don't know if that is the reaction for most of us. It was not my initial reaction.

Worship is a lot more than just going to church, but that is an essential part of worship. You already know how essential music is to my life. I was raised on the hymns. I know them all by heart.

Starting with my attendance at the "Park House," meaningful worship consisted of the shorter songs, still sung in so many churches. I once reached a point where I didn't care if I ever sang another hymn in church. It wasn't that the hymns were bad, I just found the new music very meaningful. God's presence filled the place where these songs were directed to Him.

There was a great deluge of new music. There were Musicians, Psalmists, Poets, Lyricists, Arrangers, and Worshippers that created a whole different phenomenon in our approach to God, in our approach to worship, and in church life. It was not always a smooth transition. Can you imagine the shock and horror the first time anyone dared sing any song, other than one of the songs of David, in the synagogue?

I believe it was an outpouring of the music of heaven coming to earth. (Yes, I believe the hymns, and the classics, and the good music of every generation is sung in heaven.)

There is a big difference when a worshipper steps to a microphone, rather than just a singer/performer, and the people in an audience know the difference.

I think it is possible that the greatest music *ever,* is *still to be written.* I hope that challenges you, that somewhere there is a young person, an old person, or a combination of the two, that wants to hear from heaven, that has the musical skills to write and arrange.

A few years ago I worked the weekend shift. I got my 40 hours in over Friday, Saturday, and Sunday nights. I had time for a cup of coffee after work. Then I was off to a church that ran five services on the weekend.

I attended the early, traditional service. Hymns were sung. The service was packed, and not just with the older crowd. (This was the church that provided the minister and a pianist for Jon's funeral. Even the piano player, and the selections, were perfect.)

They have a pipe organ that reaches up to heaven itself. They have a full choir. Some Sundays they have a full orchestra. I sat way up in the balcony. When God's presence filled the building, I wanted to sense The Presence first. Some Sundays I arrived early. I could sense God's presence before any activity took place.

A lot of the choir and orchestral music is majestic, with anthems, and praise. I found it very inspirational, inspiring. It ministered to my soul.

I have a lot to say about worship. Most of it I am going to save for another time. As long as corporate worship comes from the heart, has truth to it, and can be sung by a corporate crowd, it can be meaningful.

Philippians 4:6 says,..."In everything by prayer and supplication with thanksgiving, let your requests be made known to God." Psalm 100 tells us to "Come before him with joyful singing, v1, Enter His gates with thanksgiving, and His courts with praise, v1.

Gratitude is a big part of worship. Even in your darkest hour, look for the good. Thank God for the good He is doing that you can not see. There is always something you *can* see that will cause you to give thanks.

Psalm 22:3..." Oh thou that inhabitest the praises of Israel. (KJV.) The first meaning of the word inhabit is to sit down. It also means to dwell, and to ambush in quiet. When we worship, God comes to sit down with us. He quietly ambushes us!

God's goodness, power, and love is beyond comprehension. Some of His attributes are expressed back to us as we worship. His presence does far more than just make us feel good. When we are in his presence, He lets us know who He is. You learn a lot more about someone if you meet them and talk to them, than you do by only reading what they wrote.

God's presence confirms to us what we read about what He wrote.

This is why I go to church and worship:

FOR YOU

For You, For Your House, For Your Name,
We Come.
For You, For Your Word, For Your Name,
And for Your Kingdom.

For You, a House of Worship, For You,
a House of Prayer.
We Come to Give Your Honor, Show Your Power
Everywhere.

For You, For Your House, For Your Name,
We Come.
For You, For Your Word, For Your Name,
And for Your Kingdom.

Give us the Heart of those who Worship, And we will
Give You Praise.
We will Enter in Your Presence Each and
Every Day.

Drive away all that is useless, We will hold to
What is Good.
Grace and Truth to Rule our Heart, May Your Ways
be Understood.

For You who Comes to Meet us, Give Ear to what
we Pray.
We humbly ask that You Would Dwell, Show Your Glory
Here Today.

Show Your Glory, Show Your Glory, Show Your Glory in
This Place.

For You, For Your House, for Your Name,
We Come

For You, For Your Work, For Your Name, And for Your Kingdom.

David knew how to worship. He probably understood its value, and importance, more that anyone who ever lived. He had a choir of 4000 worshippers, with instruments, (1 Chronicles 23:5.) God simply honors, and responds to, genuine corporate worship.

Fill your heart and soul with good music. Saul was troubled, often. David was a skilled musician. He played for Saul. It made a great difference. Sometimes I am in the mood for the soothing mellow songs of John Michael Talbot. Sometimes I am in the mood for something less soothing. I have some worship music that is "roll down the windows, turn the volume, and let it rip."

CHAPTER TWENTY-EIGHT | THE PRESENCE OF GOD

NUMBER 4

THE PRESENCE OF GOD

Value and covet the Presence of God. I paraphrase what Moses told God in Exodus 33:15, If Your presence does not go with us, we do not want to go. We know Moses was in God's presence on the mountain. When he came down from the mountain his face glowed, Exodus 34:31. He put a veil over his face.

Isaiah 60:1, "Arise, shine; for your light has come, And the glory of the Lord has risen upon you. James 4:8, Draw near to God and He will draw near to you."

We already started this subject in the last chapter. Worship and The Presence of God are not meant be exclusive.

We were created to know God and to know His love. We were created to experience Him. This section is not meant to replace the Word of the Lord, or Worship. It is a result of the Word of the Lord and Worship. It is the result of Crying Out To God.

The presence of God will melt your heart, bring you to your knees, sometimes face down on the floor, will bring tears to your eyes. The presence of God will make clear to you the Love of God. There is a sweetness to the presence of God. You certainly are going to realize that He is Good. In His presence is fullness of joy. His presence can heal you.

Sometimes there is an awe inspiring, sense of the Holiness of God, of His Greatness, of His Lordship, of His Majesty, and we are left silent, still, and in wonder.

God's presence is not restricted to our initiation. It is still very special to me when I am aware that God does the initiating, when God speaks first, when I sense that He is there, and I have done nothing to make it happen. (I was just sitting there, minding my own business, when God…)

The outline of what I am going to share in the last four chapters of the book came to me when (literally) "I was just sitting there minding my own business." I was actually watching a scientific documentary (that is a once in a lifetime experience) on TV.

When I type the Presence of God on my computer, it wants to auto correct to "Present" of God. That is a good description. When I type in the word God, it wants to auto correct and not capitalize the word God. In this case, it needs its soul restored.

We don't have to ask for the presence of God. His presence is more of a result: When we genuinely Worship, when we Read The Word of God, When we Cry Out To Him, when He knows the direction of our life is toward Him, and not away from Him, we will experience His presence. When He initiates, sometimes He just wants to talk. It's why we were created.

It is impossible to overstate the importance, and the goodness of the Presence of God. Psalm 16:11, "In Thy presence is fullness of joy; In Thy right hand there are pleasures forever." Jesus is at the right hand of God. He represents the Love, Forgiveness, Acceptance, Mercy, Grace, Truth, the Joy and Peace, found in the Kingdom

Of God. The Presence of God heals. His presence can do wonders for the soul, the spirit, the outlook.

I was at an airport, trying to arrange a standby flight. An old friend called. We had not had any communication in years. It was great to hear from him. It was a good day, and a good week, even before he called. Hearing his voice was a special treat.

The presence of God has an even greater, more pleasant, profound effect on us than hearing from an old friend. I told my friend that he had made my day, even my week. (Hopefully it has not been years since you experienced God's presence) the presence of God can "Make our Day."

I used to hear a lot of teaching in opposition to this chapter, that we shouldn't just ask for "feel good" moments in our relationship with God. That idea pretty much missed the whole point of the Presence of God. His presence is not just a feeling. It is a valuable part of the miraculous relationship God has chosen to have with us. I want to be sensitive, to know, and appreciate, and never take for granted, His presence.

It's good to say, "God, are you here?" and know immediately, that He is.

CHAPTER TWENTY-NINE | FIND A PLACE

NUMBER 5

FIND A PLACE

1 Chronicles 17:16, "Then David the King went in and sat before the Lord..." Everyone needs a place, (and a time, if possible) where God can find us. Is there a place (and a time) where we anticipate, and expect His presence? Look up the words to Ralph Carmichael 's song *A Quiet Place*. It has been a favorite of mine since the first time I heard it.

There also is a place for special occasions. Israel had three main feasts to observe every year. I have adopted my own version of that. I try to do three special things each year to strengthen my relationship with God. Sometimes it's Kansas City. Sometimes its camp. I have gone to camp during the off season when no one was there. I once found a Catholic retreat center that I went to a few times. Sometimes I take an extra amount of time during a week without going anywhere special.

There is a lake near to where I live. That is true for everyone in Minnesota. It's beautiful. I walk around that lake. It has replaced the 1.4 mile square of my old neighborhood. It's a longer walk. I have more things that need prayer. It has been one of my favorite places in the earth since I was a teenager.

My deck is also good for more than just baseball. Baseball, and talking to God, talk about a match made in heaven!

I went to a special place, to a mountain, to write this book. The mountain had a serious fire not that long ago. I figured the parallel of a burned out mountain, and the subject of a burned out soul, would be conducive to writing. Yes, it is one of my favorite places on the earth.

I mentioned about the enthusiasm of going to church to hear what the minister is going to say. Church is not the only location for that. I want to go to "my place" to hear the footsteps of God, to have Him ambush me with His presence, or better yet, to find out He got there before I did.

MY FAVORITE PLACE

Lord you see right through my outer shell.
You know if all my heart is well.
My inner life your spirit sees,
May no evil way be found in me.

I want to know you God
And the wonder of your ways,
The goodness of hour heart
And all the words you say.

Oh purify my life today
That I may see You as I pray.
As a child I will look to You
To see the mighty things that you can do.

I want to know you God
And the wonder of your ways,
The goodness of your heart
And all the words you say.

Oh Lord declare your name to me,
And I will bow to worship Thee.
I run to find my favorite place
Where I can see you face to face

CHAPTER THIRTY | MAKE A LIST

NUMBER 6

MAKE A LIST

Check it more than twice.

I've told you about a list I made for my prayer walk years ago. Just two months ago I made a new one. I made a list of seven things. I will keep track. If I am serious about the list, I will take more than prayer/crying out to God. It will also take action on my part.

Anything we ask for, that is of significance, will need follow through on our part. God is not going to do everything for us, without our participation. We will need to take responsibility to implement what He communicates to us.

Make a list of what you are thinking. Make a list of your emotions, of how you feel, or how you don't feel. One of easiest indicators that your soul (your heart, your human spirit) is in trouble, is if you have no emotions. As time goes on, look at your list to see what has changed.

Put your questions on your list. No one has ever figured everything out, about God. No one has all of the answers. God does want to help us understand Him. He does want to reveal His nature, His character, and His heart.

Over time, review your list. See where God has helped you.

Most importantly, your list needs to include specific, short statements. It should include the things you want to change.

Be specific. Again, when you are in a state of desperation, you start with a cry for help. Then graduate. Don't pray the general formulaic prayers. You know the ones I mean: Dear God, help me to be a better person. Dear God, help our family. Dear God, help our country. Dear God help me to be a better parent/employee/ spouse/boss…etc." To each of these generalities, I would ask the question, "How? Or in what area?"

Are you asking God for more income? How much? As for parenting, are you asking for more patience, or for more insight into how to motivate junior to adopt a specific action or attitude?

The list you make should be measurable. Can progress be measured or defined? Adjust your list as needed. Be sure to give God thanks for His help.

At Christmas I ask my kids to make their own lists. The lists I make, and the ones I ask them to make, include short and long term *needs and desires*. We don't ask God to only fix the broken things. Psalm 37:4: "Delight yourself in the Lord; and He will give you the desires of your heart." Psalm 37:23: "The steps of a good man are established by the Lord."

You may have to write down goals each year for your work. They become part of your annual review at the end of the year. For us to do the same, to make a list for our own life, seems like a good idea.

I don't know how most people write books. I made an outline, awhile ago. I carried most of the book around with me, in my head, for a long time. When I began to write, I had to make lists, pages and pages of them, to help me not forget information as I went along. I made lists as ideas came in to my head, to include them as well. Then I went back through my lists, and as I typed the ideas in to the narrative, I wrote OK beside each completed item.

I do not speak fluent emoji. Truth be known, I don't speak emoji at all. If you do, put your favorite emoji, and a Thank You Lord, beside each completed item on your list.

Modify your lists. You will add some items, and say to yourself, "Why didn't I think of that before?

WHAT WILL GOD PUT ON YOUR LIST, that is more than you hoped for, that you were not expecting, that is a complete surprise?

CHAPTER THIRTY-ONE | NO DETOURS

I AM SURE EVERY STATE HAS its own unique sayings. When I was a teenager there was a saying about high school sports. In Minnesota there were two high school sports, hockey, and everything else. That has changed over the years as other athletic programs have become more prominent.

In the Twin Cities it is said that there are two seasons, winter, and road repair. We don't have enough roads. Like many cities, repairs can lag behind the needs. In our state, there are massive lists of current projects, and projects still waiting. Everyone dreads the detour signs that accompany the road repairs.

I purpose to keep you out of the detours. Detours are not always easy to follow and are not always clearly posted. Sometimes is seems almost impossible to get back to where you were. At different times Peggy and I have said, "How do we get this show back on the road? How do we get the train on the tracks? How do we get our ducks in a row?"`

Even when you are doing everything right, even when your soul is in a state of restoration, punches are still going to be thrown at you. I want you to be able to deflect them. I don't want them to knock you down.

One of the big issues in the National Football League of late, is the concussion protocol. Due to revelations of historical concussions, the league is taking extra precautions. Sometimes, just like a mandatory eight count in boxing, a football player has to sit out seven days for a concussion.

You don't want to be sidelined. You don't want to be stuck, back down in the pit.

There is the story of the salesman who comes to a new job interview, claiming ten years of experience. The interviewer asks the question, "Do you have ten years of experience, or one year's experience, ten times?"

You don't want to be on a continuous cycle of in the pit, out of the pit, in the pit, out of the pit. You don't want to be knocked out, face down on the canvas, restored, only to find yourself all too soon, face down on the canvas.

We don't want to be detoured to the right or to the left. We want be able to obey the voice that says, "This is the way, Walk in it."" Isaiah 30:21.

We have traditions at Christmas time. Both Peggy and I grew up opening presents on Christmas Eve. We have always followed that tradition. One year when the kids were a whole lot younger, we went out to get pizza in the middle of the afternoon, Christmas Eve Day.

As the kids grew, and the appetite became more refined we developed a tradition of going to the same restaurant for a Christmas Eve, late afternoon dinner. Before dinner, as many of us whose schedules allow, go to one of the many Christmas Eve services at the church with the massive pipe organ.

I have always read the Christmas Story as part of our pre-present opening celebration. Years ago, I started the tradition of giving the kids a Christmas message from dad.

The next four chapters are what I gave them as this year's Christmas message. No, I did not read four chapters of a book to them. I just gave them the four ideas as an outline.

As you "Cry Out To God," there are four things I encourage you to pray every day. Apply these four things to every item on your list, as you ask God to help you in all of the different designations.

I also believe that God will use these to help you stay out of the pit, to stay up off the canvas. We have to have a plan. Avoiding the detours will not happen without a plan. There are no shortcuts.

Boxers endure grueling workouts. Boxing is an extremely tiring endeavor. When you see two boxers tangled up during the fight, it is for one of two reasons. One of the boxers is trying to avoid getting hit by his opponent, or they are both simply too tired to separate, and throw punches.

I think the man who was just "trying to make the mortgage" was in the ring, but flat footed, not up on his toes, bouncing around. You don't want to become "weary in well doing," Galatians 6:9, KJV. You want be able to stay on "The Path Of Life."

As I go to the next four chapters, I am not saying, "Pray only, these four things." They are not to replace the needs of worship, or anything else. They will be part of your prayer, not the whole prayer. Sometimes during the day, you might ask for the four, all at once, with nothing added. Then later in the day, you many dwell on them individually.

There are four things to pray every day. I believe they are all related. I believe we need all four. Here they are:

PART FIVE

POINT OF NO RETURN

CHAPTER THIRTY-TWO | TOUCH MY HEART

NUMBER ONE: "CRY OUT TO GOD"

TOUCH MY HEART

I use the term, "Cry Out To God," not as a replacement for the word prayer, but to help explain what I mean by the word prayer. I have already talked about moving away from using generic terms when we pray. Life has serious issues. We have real needs and exciting plans. We are not asking for lollipops and rainbows. At least I hope we're not.

Whether or not our prayers are answered, matters. Look at the prayers in the Psalms. There is a lot of angst, a lot of desperation, a lot of emotion. Look at the prayer of Jesus in the garden of Gethsemane, from Luke 22:44, "And being in agony, He was praying very fervently; and His sweat became like drops of blood, falling down upon the ground."

I use the term, "Cry Out To God," to denote sincerity, intensity, raw emotion, earnestness. "....the effectual fervent prayer of a righteous man availeth much," James 5:16.

Cleland B. McAfee said in the song,

Near To The Heart Of God

"There is a place of quiet rest, Near to the Heart of God." Long before we go places we shouldn't go, or do things we shouldn't do, or buy things we should't buy, there is a struggle with the heart. "Keep thy heart with all diligence; for out of it are the issues of life." Proverbs 4:23, KJV.

The struggle for control of the heart is real for every human being. There is the plea of every generation of Proverbs 23:26, "My son, give me your heart." Of course we understand this to also be the plea of God, "My son, give me your heart." The Cares Of Life tug at our heart.

My understanding for this chapter is that you have already given God your heart, that you are looking for ways to please Him, not to defy Him, that you want His blessing, rather than trying to escape His gaze while you try to go astray.

OPEN WIDE THE DOOR

I open wide the door.
Don't stand knocking any more.
I need the sweetness of your voice.
Your completeness is my choice.

I cry to you with all my heart.
I will love you not in part.
To know you as I've never known you before,
I open wide the door.

"The soul of Jonathan (Saul's son) was knit to the soul of David." 1 Samuel 18:1. Some of the meanings of the word knit, are to tie, or to join together.

It is a very good, but also serious thing to ask God to "Touch My Heart." When we say to God, "Touch My Heart," we are not asking for a mere emotional lift for something that will make us feel better for a moment. We are asking God to change our life.

We are asking God to knit our heart with His. We are asking God to join our heart together with His. We are not just asking to be near His heart, but to make our hearts one. When we say, Touch My Heart, the question could be, "Touch my heart, how, or with what? The answer is Touch My Heart, with your heart.

As we ask God to perform miracles, to make dramatic changes, as we pray through our lists, we can keep our heart in the right place, keep our motives pure, keep our heart pure. "Blessed are the pure in heart, for they shall see God." Matthew 5:8. "With my whole heart have I sought Thee." Psalm 119:10. "Thy Word have I treasured in my heart, that I may not sin against Thee." Psalm 119:11.

If you ask God to "Touch Your Heart," don't be surprised if you sense Him asking, "Are you sure about this? Is this what you really want? " If the question is yes, it gives God freedom in, and over our lives. Every Christian eventually comes to a decision about the "Lordship" of Christ. Sometime after he becomes the Savior of our life, we come to the "fork in the road'"decision. Am I willing to make Him the Lord of my Life?

Once again, for this chapter, I believe that you have already said "Yes" to the Lordship of Christ somewhere in your spiritual journey. I also believe that when we
sincerely pray, "Touch My Heart," it may open up a completely new avenue in life. God may bring to your heart something that has never crossed your mind. Or, He may stir something in you that you thought had passed, never to be revived. These will not be bad things.

Paul said in 1 Corinthians 15:31, "I die daily." There are many possible meanings to this statement. Even the best of us, with the best motivation, fight with our own heart.

There's so sense in beating ourselves to a pulp. The best way to keep our heart in a good place is to genuinely say, every day, "Dear God, Touch My Heart."

The best thing we can do for ourselves, is to be aligned with the purpose and plan of God. When we say, "Touch My Heart," we will become more aware of those purposes and plans, and then, how they relate to our life. Let the words of my mouth and the meditation of my heart be accepted in Thy sight…Psalm 19:14.

CHAPTER THIRTY-THREE | FILL MY SPIRIT

NUMBER TWO: "CRY OUT TO GOD"

FILL MY SPIRIT

If your soul is in shambles, you have no dreams. Whatever dreams you once had seem like a distant, ancient memory, lying in a heap of ashes.

Contrast that with 2 Samuel 6:16, "Then it happened as the ark of the Lord came in to the city of David......and saw David leaping and dancing before the Lord..." Or Acts 3:8, "And with a leap, he stood upright and began to walk, and he entered the temple with them, walking and leaping and praising God" (I don't think leaping was allowed in the temple in those days.)

A side note. I once saw Phil Driscoll, another famous trumpeter, with a singing voice like Joe Cocker, in concert. He told of his thought to play a certain song in a church concert. He said to God, "If I play that song, they'll throw me out of here". Mr. Driscoll said, God told him," That's OK, they threw me out of here a long time ago." The pharisees were always trying to throw Jesus' people out of the temple/synagogue.

The cause for celebration in the two verses above was: The Ark of the Lord, the place of the presence of God, had returned home. The other was, the man leaping, seconds before, was lame. God wants to turn your ***heap of ashes*** in to a ***leap of praise.***

"He brought me out of the pit of destruction, out of the miry clay: and he set my feet upon a rock, making my footsteps firm. And He put a new song in my mouth, a song of praise to our God..." Psalm 40: 2-3. (God) "Who redeems your life from the pit; Who crowns you with loving kindness and compassion; Who satisfies your years with good things, so that your youth is renewed like the eagles," Psalm 103:4-5.

Jesus said, "I came that they might have life, and have it abundantly," John 10:10.

It is time to dream again. It may be time to resurrect the old dreams. God may want to give you brand new dreams. It is even possible that He might be in the process of radically changing your life.

When all of the calamity came to Job, he went and sat among the ashes Job 2:8. Arise from the ashes. Get up from your grave. Come to life. God's Spirit is in you. When you think you gave been abandoned, neglected, or forgotten, God says, "I have inscribed you on the palms of my hands, Isaiah 49:16." " I will never desert you, nor will I ever forsake you", Hebrews 13:5.

When we think of the term "Fill My Spirit," thoughts of the fruits of the Spirit, and the gifts of the Spirit immediately come to mind. Those are great, and of great importance and blessing, but they are not the subject of this book.

I am talking about the contrast found in Proverbs 17:22, "A joyful heart is good medicine, but a broken spirit dries up the bones. Proverbs 18:14,..."but a wounded spirit who can bear?" Sometimes a grouchy person is told, "Quit being such a bear."

It is confession time. I have a ways to go on this subject. I am the stoic. I am the arms folded person. I was not born leaping and dancing. I was not born "doing the motions." That does not excuse me, I am just letting you know my starting point.

When you watch football on television, before the game, you see team mates, sometimes in close proximity to one another, jumping up and down, with excitement, with anticipation, with enthusiasm.

Jon was three years old. It was Christmas. He was the most excited I have ever seen any one, in my entire life, to this day. He literally, was jumping up and down, all over the house, yelling at the top of his lungs, "It's Tristmas! It's Tristmas! It's Tristmas!" (He was three.) That is what I mean by "Fill My Spirit." One of the presents Jon received that year was the little plastic golf club set that, years later, Erik used for target practice.

Heaven is a place of great joy, overwhelming, beyond the imagination, joy. In 2 Corinthians 2:9 Paul quotes Isaiah 64:4, "… Eye hath not seen, nor ear heard, neither have entered in to the heart of man, the things which God hath prepared for them that love Him." Verses 10-12 continue, "but God hath revealed them to us by His Spirit; for the Spirit searcheth all things, yea, the deep things of God. For what man knoweth the things of a man, but the Spirit of God. Now we have received, not the spirit of the world, but the Spirit which is of God; that we might know the things that are freely given to us of God." (KJV)

There is some debate that this refers to heaven. (The things he has prepared.) That is possible. I think that the whole context makes it very clear, that these words refer to more than heaven. God wants to fill our spirit with His plans, before it enters our heart, our ears, or before we see the plan with our eyes. Where is the man, who is so excited with the plan of God, that he is jumping up and down all over his house, yelling at the top of his lungs, metaphorically, "It's Tristmas! It's Tristmas! It's Tristmas!"

These verses tell us God wants to reveal to our spirit, from His Spirit, the things that are freely given to us of God. This is what I mean by, "Fill My Spirit." Is this more important than the fruit or the gifts?

We are not limited to only one choice here. Imagine God saying, "You can have the fruits/gifts, but no excitement is allowed, or conversely, you can have enthusiasm, but you will be fruitless and powerless."

We have a great piece of artwork in our home. It shows Jesus in a big circle with children. They are involved in some sort of a celebratory dance. There are others in the background, some with arms folded, looking on, with unhidden disapproval.

God wants to Restore Your Soul, and Fill Your Spirit….."Now to Him who is able to do exceeding abundantly beyond all that we ask or think, according to the power that works within us," Ephesians 3:20.

Am I willing to embrace this promise? Am I willing to believe this is possible? Am I willing to believe God loves me enough to do this? Am I willing to allow God, or do I genuinely want God to do this?

God's plan is for His work to energize us, not point us back to the pit. In some corners we have been sold a bad bill of goods that says the plan of God will weigh us down, burn us out, and make our lives miserable. We've bought the rotten bag of seed that says the abundant life is not really for those who are truly serving God. Let God refresh your spirit, "Fill Your Spirit."

Dear God, bring life to the dead bones of my spirit. Cause my spirit to come up out the grave. Bring life, bring anticipation, bring genuine faith, bring joy, bring enthusiasm, bring revelation, bring purpose, bring value, bring intensity, bring determination, bring obedience, bring excitement.

And so, we bring the Spirit of God to our lists. Do you feel better about your lists than you did ten minutes ago? Can you see God filling your spirit with promises of things yet to come, things that will enter your mind, soon to be seen by your eyes?

CHAPTER THIRTY-FOUR | QUICKEN MY MIND

NUMBER THREE: "CRY OUT TO GOD"

QUICKEN MY MIND

Quicken. That is an old word. (That's OK. I'm not a kid.) I think I chose it from the verse, memorized as a kid, Hebrews 4:12, "For the word of God is quick, and powerful…" Quick means to live, or life. God's Word is alive. Jesus said, My words are spirit and they are life.

God's Word is **LIFE.** It will bring life to our mind, not confusion. How often do we approach a subject feeling muddled, indecisive, directionless, maybe even hopeless? I have said, way too many times. I don't know what to do. I don't have an answer. God wants to "Quicken Our Mind." Another way of saying this, is this simple request:

TALK TO ME

What I am really saying is, **"Dear God, Please Talk To Me."**

Something happens that is different when you read Scripture, than when you read Shakespeare. (Me thinks thou are overrated too much.) We know that God talks to us through Scripture, but He is not limited to speaking only during Bible reading. We know He speaks to us when we "Cry out to Him." We want our mind to be in a place, where God feels at home, where He feels welcome to *start* a conversation anytime.

We are bombarded with battles, the battle of the bands, the battle of the sexes, the Battle of Bull Run, even Battlestar Galatica. The biggest battle we have is for the battle of our mind. This goes on every day. Do we think in these terms, that it goes on every day? I have two ways that describe some of the items of the battle. One is a poem. The other is a song. First the poem:

I know all the batting averages
Of everyone at bat.
I know all the pitchers E.R.A.'s
And every other stat.
I know every game, who won, who lost,
This year and long before.
I can tell you all the players
From the team in '64.

I know every celebrity,
Who they've dated, who they've seen.
I know all their glossy photographs
In every magazine.
I know the lines from all the movies
And who won the big award.
I can tell you who is interesting
And who just leaves me bored.

I know all the right investments.
I know how to make a buck.
I know when to take the punches.
I know just when to duck.
I know all the brand new recipes.
I can make a great souffle.
You can find me at the health club.
I know just what I should weigh.

It can be good to have a hobby.
It can be good to play and laugh.

It is good to be on fire
And to burn away the chaff.

Does our culture take away our time,
Too much glitz and shallow charm?
Does it leave our heart and spirit cold?
Does it leave us just lukewarm?

The song:

YOU CALLED

I don't care that much for silver
And I already own all your gold.
It's not the homes and the clothes,
Or the cars that you drive,
For everything that you own
Will one day be sold.

You called and no one answered
You spoke and no one heard.
There is nothing more important
Than your Word.

I don't need just another voice
That is skillfully trained
Or the appearance
Of a fashion magazine.

I'm not impressed by mere talent
Or with the games that you play

Or the things that you watch on the screen.

You called and no one answered.
You spoke and no one heard.
There is nothing more important
Than your Word.

I can bless a life that's not too busy for me.
I can use anyone who does not want to be a star.
I love a hungry heart that has
Not fully arrived.
I look for people who want to become
So much more than they are.

You called and no one answered.
You spoke and no one heard
There is nothing more important
Than your word.

I would that all my sons were prophets
That my daughter dwell in the courts of her king.

I included the above, to illustrate the struggle we face. I think the biggest battle any one faces is the battle for the mind. In a previous chapter I made only a partial list of the responsibilities we face as we attack the "Cares Of Life." We are confronted with an even larger list when we consider all the things that come across our mind in one single day.

Our mind is where we decide what is important. The decisions we make with our mind determine whether we win or lose, rise or fall, fight or surrender, whether we go forward at all, or tread water, hoping to just stay alive, whether we go forward with faith or fear.

The decisions we make with our mind determine the direction we take. What we feed, water, and pamper determines the thought patterns, and eventual actions we take.

I will try to be very careful here: It is not evil, or inherently wrong to have what could be considered "nonspiritual" thoughts in our mind. I did not sense God asking me to totally give up baseball as He was restoring my soul. (Is it possible that baseball is included in the list of "every good..and perfect gift is from above, coming down from the Father of Lights"? from James 1:17. I think Psalm 19:14 gives an overall view of what I am trying to say. I think all thoughts and speech is included in this verse: "Let the words of my mouth and the meditation of my heart be acceptable in Thy sight."

I think you can take your son fishing, talk about bait, worms, and minnows without being in danger. When he is in Sunday school, and the subject of "fishers of men," comes up, he might be one leg up on his friends in understanding the concept.

Another way to look at this subject: Overall, is our mind committed to God, so that all of our thoughts receive His favor, or are we so compromised by the pull of our surroundings and The Cares Of Life, that God would have to drag us out of our burning city, "kicking and screaming," (my words) like Lot, to escape destruction,? (from Genesis 19) Our minds will determine whether we are left with a blessing, or a pillar of salt.

We'll talk about not setting "worthless things before our eyes," Psalm 101:3, in the next chapter. The KJV uses the term wicked. Some meanings of this word are, worthless, without profit, or evil. Is it possible that this is a challenge for our mind as well?

Again, for this chapter, I am going to consider that you want your mind to be in the right place, that you want God's help, that you want Him to "Talk To You."

When you buy a car, especially if it is a brand or model you have not owned recently, all of a sudden you start to notice how many of "your cars" are on the road. Once you start crying out to God, to start bringing life to your mind, it is amazing to see how many Scriptures are dedicated to our thoughts, our minds, and our priorities. Apply your prayers for your mind to your lists. Ask God what He thinks about each item. Ask Him how He wants you to think about each item. If it hasn't already, your attention will soon be turned to the subjects of wisdom and understanding.

"For My thoughts are not your thoughts, Neither are your ways My ways, declares the Lord. For as the heavens are higher than the earth, so are My ways higher than your ways, and My thoughts than your thoughts," Isaiah 55:8-9.

God is never held to "conventional wisdom." or conventional anything else, for that matter. Paul said, "Oh, the depth of the riches both of the wisdom and knowledge of God! How unsearchable are His judgements and unfathomable His ways. For who has known the mind of the Lord…?"

Steve Allen was a famous talk show host, musician (he wrote over 4000 songs,) comedian and author. He once wrote a book called, "Explaining China." He said the title was part tongue in cheek, as in, could one "Explain China, " in only one book. Well, we are never going to be able to "Explain God," or understand all that He is, or all that He knows, in any amount of books. I believe the statement, His ways are "past finding out." Romans 11:33 KJV, applies all to of eternity, that trillions of years in to eternity, we will discover new things about God, (not new to Him, but new to us.)

For we mortals, trying to "figure it out," God does want us to understand Him, as it pertains to our human existence. "Let not a wise man boast in his wisdom (man's wisdom, conventional wisdom, my words) and let not the mighty man boast of his might, let not a rich man boast of his riches; but let him who boasts, boast of this, that he knows and understands Me, that I am the Lord who exercises loving kindness, justice, and righteousness on earth; for I delight in these things..." Jeremiah 9:23-24. It is worth a separate study, just to take notice of the things that delight God.

God wants us to know and understand him. He wants us to have wisdom. Wisdom means to be wise in mind, even skillful.

"Wisdom is the principle thing; therefore get wisdom, and with all thy getting, get understanding," Proverbs 4:7, KJV. "Be not wise in your own eyes (conventional wisdom,) fear the Lord and turn away from evil," Proverbs 3:7. "The fear of the Lord is the beginning of wisdom, and the knowledge of the Holy One is understanding," Proverbs 9:10/Psalm 111:10. In Genesis chapter 39, Joseph is propositioned by his master's wife. His response: "How could I do this great evil, and sin against God?", verse 9.

Let me try to summarize at least some of this. God wants us to know and understand Him, and His ways. Wisdom is a term used to define God's ways, as differentiated from the normal way most men think. Wisdom comes from placing a priority on knowing God's ways. This results in us having the knowledge to choose to refrain from evil, because we have chosen wisdom.

To want God's favor and to have wisdom are two main ingredients to help us think right, and to make right choices in our actions. We can stay away from evil.

When we ask God for wisdom and understanding, when we ask God to "Quicken Our Mind," especially as it pertains to our lists, in part we are asking: "Give me guidance, instruction, direction, ideas, and confirmation. Tell me what to do. ***Talk To Me.***" Help me to know the answers to the questions of when, where, how, how much, when to press in, when to back off, went to go, when to stay." David repeatedly asked God if he should go in to battle against his enemies.

Have you ever wondered, "What goes through God's mind every day? (We know He doesn't view life in terms of twenty-four hour days like we do.) I want to know what God thinks. I want to know what He thinks about the issues that pertain to my life, what He thinks about His Kingdom on earth, and how those two planes should intersect.

I want the Wisdom of the Ages, from before time began, to make my mind alive, with new, fresh ideas (And I'm the one whose natural inclination is, "If it ain't broke, don't fix it.") I need to know more than I can summon with mere mortal intellect.

An acquaintance of mine was moving out of the country. He was my favorite barista in my favorite coffee shop, at the time. I asked him if he was "running to, or running from?" He said, "A little of both." If the overall direction of our mind is running toward God," rather than "away from Him," he will "Quicken Our Mind." This will help us to stay out of the pit, and *Up Off The Canvas.*

CHAPTER THRITY-FIVE: OPEN MY EYES

NUMBER FOUR: "CRY OUT TO GOD"

OPEN MY EYES

My favorite arrangement for my trumpet was one I put together during my Internship. It was an arrangement of the Battle Hymn Of The Republic. I don't think I changed a note of it over decades of time. The thing that caught my attention the most is the initial words of the first verse, "Mine eyes have seen the Glory." That one phrase has been a cry of ***my*** heart ever since. If we could only see one thing, that would be it, The Glory of the Lord.

We have already referenced "setting no worthless thing before our eyes," (last chapter,) and "God sees not as man sees..." from 1 Samuel, when David was chosen as the future king of Israel. If we are going to avoid the pit, we need to see what God sees. We need to avoid anything that can cause destruction.

The story was told about a man who got a new cell phone from his wife for Christmas. She called him while he was driving. and said, "Be careful, there is an item on the news about someone driving on the freeway, going the wrong direction." He said to his wife, "Oh it's worse that you think. There must be at least a hundred of them." "Seeing what God sees can keep us going in the right direction.

One episode in the Bible is a literal telling of, "Open My Eyes." Read the whole story in 2 Kings Chapter 6. The king of Aram sent a whole army to Dothan, just to destroy Elisha the prophet. (You know you are doing something right when they think it will take a whole army, just to get rid of you.) The king sent a great army with chariots and horses to surround the city. Elisha's attendant got up early in the morning, saw the situation, and was "scared to death," (my words.) He asks Elisha what to do.

Elisha told the servant, "Do not fear, for those who are with us are more than those who are with them, v16. Then Elisha prayed and said, "O Lord, I pray, Open his eyes that he may see. And the Lord opened the servant's eyes, and he saw; and behold the mountain was full of horses and chariots and fire all around Elisha." Psalm 34:7 says, "The angel of the Lord encamps around those who fear Him, and rescues them. (Another reason to depart from evil.)

I already admitted, I failed to recognize, acknowledge, or give thanks for all of the things God did, even when I was stumbling around in the ring. Even though a different course was set for my life, I don't think it was His plan for me to be face down on the canvas. I did not always see what He saw. I did not always hear what He said.

Just as God's ways are not the same as our ways, His thoughts are completely above and beyond our thoughts, so His sight is exponentially beyond our ability to see. I have maintained that about the only thing wrong with teenagers (on the rare occasion where they do anything wrong) is: They can't see far enough. They can't see how their thoughts or actions have consequences that can last forever.

One of the most poignant songs I ever heard is, *Yesterday When I Was Young*, written by Charles Aznavour and Fred Ebb. It was sung by Roy Clark. The song was sung at Mickey Mantle's funeral. I think every teenager and young adult should memorize it. The words are easy to find online.

We "adult" Christians are sometimes no different than any teenager. We don't have the ability to see into the future, to see as God sees. We haven't asked Him to "Open Our Eyes."

In the Old Testament, Israel could 'See" God's provision, and they still struggled. Exodus 13:21-22: "And the Lord was going before them as a pillar of cloud by day to lead them on the way, and pillar of fire by night to give them light, that they might travel by day and by night. (even God pulls an all nighter once in awhile) He did not take away the pillar of cloud by day, nor the pillar of fire by night, from before the people. They had a visible reminder that the mercies of God are new every morning. Lamentations 3:22-23 KJV)

God is very practical. I believe the cloud and the pillar of fire also kept them protected from the heat of the sun during the day, and the cold during the night.

Even more, they carried around a rock: "Take the rod; and you and your brother Aaron assemble the congregation and speak to the rock before their eyes, that it may yield its water. You shall thus bring forth water for them out of the rock and let the congregation and their beasts drink," Numbers 20:8. (You didn't think I was going to get through the book without at least one Numbers reference, did you?) Can you imagine Moses' checklist as he left his house (tent) each morning,? "Keys, cell phone, billfold, rock".

As we apply "Open My Eyes" to our lists, Cry Out To God, "Help me to be aware of the things in plain sight, the things you have given me for my day to day existence.

May I be grateful, and never doubt that you are here, taking care of me."

Peggy does a great job of encouraging me to "enjoy the journey." God is so good, to supply us with more than just the "bare necessities." His guarantee to Israel was a promised land, full of milk and honey. I have always tried to not overdramatize, or over exaggerate, meanings or symbols from the Old Testament. Does it sound plausible that the Milk could refer to an essential? That the Honey could refer to the unessential, the blessing of God, even sweetness? I do believe that God wants to bring what we would call "sweetness' to our lives. Then, the other obvious cry, "Dear God, what do you see that I do not see? What have you prepared that I do not know?

Psalm 121:1-7, "I will lift up my eyes to the mountains; From whence shall my help come? My help comes from the Lord, Who made heaven and earth. He will not allow your foot to slip; He who keeps you will not slumber. Behold, He who keeps Israel will neither slumber nor sleep. The Lord is your keeper; the Lord is your shade on your right hand. The sun will not smite you by day, nor the moon by night. The Lord will protect you from evil; He will keep your soul."

ENCORE?

I HAVE TALKED A LOT ABOUT being a Christian. To become a Christian is not a difficult transition. The difficulty was the crucifixion of Jesus, on the cross. All that is needed is a Simple, genuine prayer:

"Cry out to God with me, "Dear God, please forgive me, for everything. Come into my life, (heart, spirit, mind, eyes.) Redeem, and Restore my soul. Show me how to live. Thank You. Amen!"

Detroit: I'm in your corner, I'm pullin' for ya.

Are you ready to lace them up (the gloves) and "go the distance?"

I tend to recoil, when I go to the grocery store, or the bank, and the cashier/teller hits me up for the latest fundraiser for some organization. I realize they are told to do this, and they may not be any more excited about it than I am. So, if this is the case for you as well, you can skip the next paragraphs.

It will come as no surprise that I am deeply moved by the drug crisis that has gripped our country. So many organizations are doing all they can to alleviate this. Almost sixty years ago a young minister went to New York City. His name was David Wilkerson. He started a program called Teen Challenge. It is a faith based recovery program/ministry for drugs and alcohol.

Today, there are Teen Challenge Centers all over the country. They have programs for teen men and women, as well as for adult men and women. Not all centers include all four programs. These centers are faith based programs. Nothing is perfect, but the overall retention rate (those who remain free form drugs and alcohol) is statistically much higher that conventional programs.

Sometimes a judge or a court is willing to consider Teen Challenge as an alternative to jail or prison. You can always make an appeal.

I am especially aware of the outstanding work that takes place at the Minnesota Teen Challenge. (Jon would not go there.)

If you need to, consider Teen Challenge as an avenue of restoration.

If you can, consider a financial gift to Minnesota Teen Challenge, or a Teen Challenge Center near you. Those in a Teen Challenge program, and those who graduate from a program need mentors, and eventually someone to "'take a chance" on them by providing employment. You can contact a local Teen Challenge office to get more information.

Thank you.

Made in the USA
Middletown, DE
05 August 2022